EVERY STEP IS A GIFT

EVERY STEP IS A GIFT:

CAREGIVING, ENDURANCE, AND THE PATH TO GRATITUDE

JOSH LASKY

NEW DEGREE PRESS

COPYRIGHT © 2020 JOSH LASKY

All rights reserved.

EVERY STEP IS A GIFT

Caregiving, Endurance, and the Path to Gratitude

ISBN   978-1-63676-581-5   *Paperback*

978-1-63676-201-2   *Kindle Ebook*

978-1-63676-202-9   *Ebook*

For Maury, Susan, Max, Kate, and Jonathan

CONTENTS

PROLOGUE   9

CHAPTER 1.   ADMISSIONS   17

CHAPTER 2.   THINGS HEADED SOUTH   27

CHAPTER 3.   OF CRAYONS AND CAMELOT   37

CHAPTER 4.   MINING TRUTHS   49

CHAPTER 5.   DESTINATION TRANSFORMED   61

CHAPTER 6.   THE DRILL...   73

CHAPTER 7.   ...AND THE SHOVEL   81

CHAPTER 8.   SILENCING ALARMS   91

CHAPTER 9.   BEYOND THE BREAKING POINT   99

CHAPTER 10.   THE TUNNEL   109

CHAPTER 11.   "THEN GO!"   123

CHAPTER 12.   ROUTINE MAINTENANCE   135

CHAPTER 13.   ONE HUNDRED PERCENT   147

CHAPTER 14.   WATCH AND LEARN   159

CHAPTER 15.   BEARING WITNESS   167

CHAPTER 16.   AND THEN RELIEF   173

CHAPTER 17.   CLAY, SILT, AND SAND   185

APPENDIX   195

ACKNOWLEDGMENTS   197

PROLOGUE

I must have gotten the call a hundred times.

It could come when I was at work, other times when I was on a first date, or occasionally in the middle of the night. No matter when it came, it always went the same: "Hi, Josh. I just wanted to let you know that your father had a fall in his room. He bumped his head against the dresser, and he had a pretty bad cut on the forehead."

The voice on the other end of the line was the charge nurse on the Five West nursing unit at the Wasserman Building of the Hebrew Home of Greater Washington. My father lived there for the last nine years of his life as he battled the ever-advancing enemy of Parkinson's disease. The degenerative condition made him a prisoner in his own body, confining him with a combination of involuntary and unpredictable tremors, fatigue, stiffness, and loss of balance and coordination.

"Thanks for letting me know. How is he feeling?" I would ask with concern, sensing the anxiousness setting into my neck and shoulders.

"He's a little shaken up, but he's alright. We used some butterfly strips to close the wound, so he most likely won't need any stitches," the nurse would say.

"I'll give him a call soon," I would respond. "Thanks for taking care of him, and thanks for letting me know." After having the conversation so many times, it was almost as if I was reading off a script, and the nurse was too, in a way. Any time a resident in long-term care has a fall, the facility is required to notify their primary family member or caregiver.

After years of this, I wondered whether being notified was actually worth it. Denial is, without a doubt, a powerful coping mechanism. To put a spin on a familiar adage, "If a father falls in his nursing home, and his son isn't notified, did it really happen?" What exactly is the value of knowing this information after dozens and dozens of falls? I already knew my father's head was badly scarred, both physically and emotionally. And I was no longer feeling the jolt of adrenaline induced by those phone calls early on in the eleven years I looked after my dad. Instead, the calls had become mundane and expected. It didn't make them any easier, though. Thinking about how accustomed I'd become to those conversations was just depressing.

Over time, though, with a mix of dread and guilt, I anticipated a different kind of phone call: the inevitable call during which I would learn that my father was dead. That was information certainly worth knowing.

***

Knowing is one of the most foundational elements of our human existence. In many ways, this book is about the power of knowing and the resulting transformation. Caregiving forces us into a position of discovering uncomfortable truths, whether or not we are prepared. In my role as my dad's caregiver, I learned more than I could have ever imagined, and often, in ways I wasn't expecting. Many caregivers are processing what they're learning through their experience. In the US alone, AARP estimates that 47.9 million people are caring for individuals over the age of eighteen as of 2020, up from 39.8 million just five years ago.[1]

I accepted the responsibility for supporting my father at a relatively young age. I was twenty-one at the time I jumped into that role, and the average age of caregivers in the US is forty-nine. The average duration of caregiving is about four and a half years, a length of time I might have anticipated when beginning to look after my father. Our journey together lasted eleven years, far longer than I could have ever anticipated.[2]

My motivations for becoming a caregiver are rooted in my identity and my upbringing. My parents had a complicated relationship, and they fought constantly while I was a child. I sensed something was always "wrong" with my family. As a result, I don't know that I ever felt like I got enough attention, or the right kind of attention, at home. In turn, I sought validation and support from other sources, seeking approval from teachers and filling nearly every stereotype of the overachiever at school.

By the time I was a teenager, I was a bit obsessive in my perfectionism. I had a hard time letting go, and an even

---

1   National Alliance for Caregiving and AARP Family *Caregiving, Caregiving in the US* 2020, May 2020, 4.

2   "Caregiver Statistics: Demographics," Family Caregiver Alliance, last modified April 17, 2019.

harder time seeing broken things remain unfixed. Shortly after my father was diagnosed with Parkinson's, he and my mother filed for divorce. I felt immense pressure to make things better. Entering high school, I tried to make the relationship with my father work after he moved out and his condition worsened, but it was terribly difficult. There was so much I had hoped to learn from him, but the example he set was woefully disappointing. I taught myself how to fashion a half-Windsor necktie knot from a book, something I should have been taught by my father, him smiling over my shoulder as we looked into a mirror. Dinners at his apartment were too often an unseasoned piece of fish overcooked on my father's beloved George Foreman Grill atop a grease-covered counter. Though my parents' custody agreement specified that my little brother and I would spend every other weekend at our father's place, those weekends were reduced to just a night or just a few hours on a Saturday or Sunday. I got the sense he didn't take fatherhood seriously, and as a result, I became less and less invested in our relationship.

Things changed, however, as I was getting ready to graduate college, when it was clear he couldn't survive without help. His ex-wife, my mother, was off the hook, and his sister was no longer able to support him. Five years my little brother's senior, I was the obvious choice to lead by doing the right thing. Could I fix my relationship with my dad? Could I fix *him*? Could I fix *myself*?

***

Over the course of supporting my father toward the end of his life, I came to the realization that my story, while unique, is also universal. I realized countless others are working to support dying parents, siblings, and friends. More than that, I realized the lessons I learned reach far beyond caregiving. Ultimately, the insights I took from my journey with my dad haven't just prepared me to be a better caregiver. They've prepared me to be a better person.

This is a story about caregiving, but caregiving in my story can be proxy for nearly any other challenge we're forced to encounter. I firmly believe that the more we are willing to embrace struggle, the stronger and more resilient we become. In some ways, I consider myself lucky to have dealt with the challenge of supporting my father early on in life. I learned lessons as a caregiver that I'll carry with me as long as I live, and I feel more prepared to take on things that might have otherwise intimidated me had I not spent just over a decade looking after my dad.

This, too, is a story about the transformative power of endurance sports, but you don't need to be an athlete to appreciate my story. It just so happens that long-distance biking and running provided fitting and illuminating analogies for my service as a caregiver. You simply cannot grit your teeth and outlast a fifty-mile run or a hundred-mile bike ride. You need to settle in. You need to find a way to get comfortable, even in discomfort. You need to weather the lows and feed off the highs. And you need to be able to breathe throughout.

The path to gratitude is different for everyone. For me, it started in a place of supreme confidence—near invincibility, really—that I was capable of anything, most certainly repairing the relationship with my dad. Almost immediately, I was humbled by the weight of caregiving. My ego was entirely replaced by helplessness and, occasionally, feelings of bitterness. Even though I had voluntarily chosen to take on the responsibility of supporting my father, I still felt at times that it was unfair. For a long time, I struggled to figure things out and suffered emotionally as a result. I had wildly high expectations for what was possible for my father's quality of life and for our relationship, and routinely those expectations were completely dashed.

But as it often does, frustration and disappointment yield new perspective. As I struggled to be a good son, I realized there were limitations for what I could do for my father. I could not suffer for him. I could not take his discomfort and experience it for him. I could not live his life for him. It took years, but I eventually found my balance in the caregiver role, and in that balance, I found a sense of purpose. Being there for a loved one, in any capacity, is a virtuous act. For those who need us, bearing witness is meaningful in and of itself. As a byproduct of that service, we come to know gratitude. I became grateful for the moments I shared with my dad, even the really hard moments, and as a result, I became grateful for so much more in my life.

PART I

CHAPTER 1

ADMISSIONS

I gazed over at my father as we rode the Metro's red line in silence. We were headed to Union Station where he'd take the Amtrak back to New Jersey. I was eagerly awaiting the moment I would watch him board the train so I could exhale for the first time in forty-eight hours.

After two days, I desperately needed to create distance between myself and my dad. I had spent more time with my father in the past two days than I had in the previous two years, and as much as I wanted it to be enjoyable, I was racked with anxiety the entire time. In my mind, I had envisioned his visit to Washington, DC would be the kind of bonding experience I had yearned for since I was thirteen, during a time when he was still healthy. Instead, the reality of the past couple of days had turned out to be more nightmare than dream, and that didn't bode well for our future together.

"How much longer until we get there?" my father asked. "My pill is starting to wear off."

"Another ten minutes," I replied. "We can grab you some water at the food court before you get on the train so you can take your meds."

"Okay, good," he said, sounding relieved. "I don't want to wait too long, otherwise I'll be stuck."

A few months prior, I had completed an application for my father to become a resident at St. Mary's Court, a 140-unit building that provided affordable housing to seniors and adults with accessibility needs. I had become familiar with the building as a volunteer, teaching a weekly current events class to residents on Thursdays during lunch. I would print out a stack of articles from the online edition of the *New York Times* and *Washington Post*, offering short narrative summaries and highlighting what I found to be interesting tidbits. Though there wasn't always lively discussion, I could always count on some smiles and nods as my students licked their thumbs and leafed through the stapled packets.

The residents at St. Mary's were wonderfully diverse, and for that reason, I could see my father fitting in well. The community was a cornucopia of racial and ethnic backgrounds, and I had overheard conversations in at least a dozen languages during my time in the building cafeteria. Residents spanned a broad spectrum of physical and cognitive abilities, and I saw various mobility devices being put to use during any one of my numerous visits. Even a few residents had Parkinson's, and they seemed to manage quite well. The community was also supported by a network of active, compassionate volunteers. The building provided two meals a day in the dining room on the ground floor, so my father wouldn't have to cook as often. This was a good thing since it was increasingly dangerous for my father to navigate the sharp edges and heat of the kitchen.

My father needed a place to live, and St. Mary's offered the right blend of freedom and support, given his needs. It also happened to be three blocks from where I was living at the time, situated just at the edge of the campus of The George Washington University (GW) where I had recently started grad school and was working part-time. Given the convenient alignment of timing and geography, St. Mary's appeared—at least on paper—to be an optimal setting for my father, and I was hoping that one of the 123 unfurnished efficiencies in the building could one day be his.

I looked over at my dad again. Though he presented much older, his sixty-two years weren't enough to meet the minimum age requirements for residency at St. Mary's. However, he was eligible to move in because of his Parkinson's disease. Having lived with it for twelve years, my father's body wore some of its unmistakable symptoms. He stared blankly and emotionlessly, slouching forward and to the side in the seat next to me. His eyes were sunk deep into his skull, encircled by dark shadows. I swallowed hard, unsettled by the fact that my father would be moving so near, should his application to St. Mary's be approved. The application required an in-person interview, and that had been the impetus for his visit to DC.

One day prior, the day of his interview, I had awoken to the rhythmic ratcheting of my father's snoring just a few feet away. I had told him to sleep in my bed, and I slept on the tiny Ikea loveseat I kept opposite the desk in my cramped bedroom. I slowly propped myself up on my elbows while the stiffness in my back prompted an involuntary wince. I managed to get to a standing position and glanced over at my father, his mouth wide open. His head jerked to the side as he snored again loudly.

One of my three roommates was up and making breakfast before heading to work. I walked toward the kitchen, my feet padding silently over the beige carpeted hallway to the edge of the tile. "Patti, thank you again," I said.

"Yeah, no problem, Josh," she replied.

Patti, a fourth-year medical student, was being gracious in the moment, though she was always quite caring. She understood what I was trying to do, and she was sympathetic. That meant absorbing the inconvenience of having yet another body taking up space in our already constrained apartment. The four of us sharing a single bathroom presented challenges without an added visitor, let alone someone who took nearly forty minutes to complete his morning routine.

"Dad, it's time to wake up," I said after returning to my room. "I've got to head to class, and you've got to start getting ready for your interview." I draped a maroon towel for him over the back of my desk chair.

"Okay," he said wearily, glancing in my direction through narrow eyes as if he had no idea where he was, as he yawned and rolled away from me.

***

A few hours later, I arrived at St. Mary's just in time to see my father walking up to the building's automatic sliding glass doors. I had asked my father to use his walker to get around during his visit, and much to my surprise, he had obliged. He had become increasingly unsteady on his feet, and I had made the request that he use the walker, for my benefit mostly. I didn't want to watch him fall anymore, at least not while stubbornly trying to walk unassisted.

We made our way through the lobby to a set of chairs upholstered in green fabric. A few minutes later, Margaret appeared at the door to her office and beckoned for my dad to join her. He slowly rose to his feet, swung the walker over to his left, and then began shuffling in her direction with a smile.

"How are you, Maury?" Margaret asked.

"Doing great," he responded dryly, disappearing inside while she closed the door behind him.

I stared ahead at the wood-paneled walls and considered the situation. It was a kind of backward college interview in which the kid was stuck in the waiting room praying the dad would say all the right things to the admissions officer. *Please don't screw this up*, I thought. But the nerves I felt in that moment weren't the kind derived from trying to will an acceptance letter into existence.

I was anxious because I knew if the interview went well, which I had expected, it would trigger a series of events with immeasurable consequences. I would move my father to Washington, DC and become his primary support structure. I would need to take on the job of keeping him clothed, fed, and seen by doctors. I would need to make sure his rent was paid. I would need to find a way to add meaning to his life as his physical abilities and his personal freedom eroded from beneath him, as though he were the inhabitant to an ever-shrinking deserted island amid a slowly rising sea. I suddenly felt my heartbeat pulsing in my neck and looked down at my hand gripped tightly around the armrest. I imagined myself completely without control in the passenger seat of a car headed toward a cliff, my foot stepping on a brake pedal that wasn't even there and trying desperately to slow the inevitable.

Thirty minutes later, Margaret opened her door and my father ambled forward behind his silver walker. "Maury is a real jokester," she said. "He'll fit in well here."

As we left the building, I turned to my father. "Sounds like it went really well, huh?"

"Yeah, it did. I like her a lot," he said. His eyes were looking down, but I could tell he wasn't focused on the ground in front of him.

I wish I knew what my dad said to convince Margaret that he was a good fit, but he wasn't exactly being forthcoming with his reactions to the interview. For most of my life, my father was never at a loss for words, but he had exceptionally few to share with me at that moment. "You okay?" I asked.

"I think so," he said. "This is going to be a big change."

That was an understatement if one ever existed. *Indeed*, I thought. A group of three students in sneakers and mesh shorts passed us on their way to the GW gym. We moved steadily in the direction of my apartment side by side, the wheels of my father's walker bouncing over the brick sidewalk.

There was uncertainty in the air around us then, and it hovered closely over us for the remainder of my father's time in DC. As the train neared Union Station, I helped my dad up out of his seat and slung his duffel bag over my shoulder. It was heavier than it should have been. The last two days had worn on me unexpectedly. I had cooked my father's meals and attempted to structure his time. In the mornings, I gave him a copy of my schedule and a list of things to do: play on my computer, watch television, explore the Foggy Bottom neighborhood, and so forth.

I left to go to work and then to class, praying he didn't get in trouble or hurt himself. The weight of that worry alone was enough to stress me out to the point where I couldn't focus, and this was only two days. I wondered if this was what it was like to care for an infant. I was exhausted both mentally and emotionally, and my back was hurting. I had just finished my undergraduate degree three months earlier, but I felt something I'd never felt before. I felt old.

When we reached the gate, I handed off my father's bags to the Amtrak porter and carefully gave my dad a very gentle hug. It was one of his "off" periods between doses of medicine, and he was unsteady at best, so I didn't want to knock him over.

"Good to spend time with you, Dad," I said. "I'll talk to you soon."

"Take care, Josh," he offered. He seemed distracted, but I knew it was because he needed to take another pill as soon as he got on the train. His tone was markedly distant, and it was clear he was mourning the life he used to have, his new reality approaching with the steadiness and inevitability of the locomotive he was riding.

I watched him shuffle away, hunched over his walker, and disappear down the escalator to the platform. "Godspeed," I whispered quietly, feeling a pang of sympathy and sadness for my father.

***

I rode the Metro back to Foggy Bottom with my forehead on the seatback in front of me and my head between my hands. I massaged my temples with my first and second fingers in a circular motion as a pathetic attempt to relax myself. It wasn't working.

Like so many instances of doing the right thing, in concept, it is admirable, even poetic. The reality, however, presents itself without regard for, and perhaps in retaliation to, our hopes and expectations. I wanted so badly to rekindle the relationship with my father, but I felt as though I had unwittingly adopted a child. I wasn't ready for a kid. Hell, I wasn't even ready for a plant. However, there was a greater problem. I was hopelessly frustrated that my father wasn't going to take directions from me even though that was, in my mind, part of the deal. I yearned for any indication that he was ready to rely on me for help and guidance. Instead, he gripped tightly to the delusion that he was still capable of making his own decisions and that he could get by on his own. The continual resistance to using his walker and the notable absence of gratitude were all the evidence I needed. I don't think I heard a "thank you" from him during our time together, and that caused me supreme disappointment.

Riding the escalator to street level out of the Foggy Bottom station, I turned and headed away from my apartment and, instead, toward a friend's place. I needed someone to talk to, though I had no idea how I was going to convey my thoughts or what kind of response I would get. At twenty-one, no one I knew had ever been a caregiver for their parent, so I continually reminded myself to temper expectations when I sought empathy, camaraderie, or life-tested insight.

A few minutes later, my friend Chris opened the door of his rowhouse to let me in. I opened my mouth to speak, but instead, I just broke down and started crying hysterically in his foyer, standing next to the roommates' three bikes piled up against the wall beneath the stairs. Chris knew about my dad, and he knew I would be hosting him for a couple of days. Without hesitation, he wrapped his arms around me and pressed my shoulders into his. I sobbed and gasped in shallow breaths, allowing myself to feel overwhelmed without resisting and hoping to flush out the anguish, fear, and helplessness of the last two days.

After half a minute, I took a single deep breath, relaxing our embrace and taking a step back. "I don't know if I can do this," I uttered softly, looking downward and slowly moving my head side to side.

"I can't imagine how tough this is going to be for you," he replied. The look in his eyes showed me just how much he wanted to understand how I felt, but it also revealed that he wouldn't be able to understand. As much as his words comforted me, his facial expression left me feeling even more isolated and more uncertain about the future.

"That's the problem," I said. "I can't either."

CHAPTER 2

THINGS HEADED SOUTH

During the four years I spent as an undergraduate at GW, I made the drive between my hometown of Cranford, New Jersey, and Washington, DC at least twenty-five times. On a good day, it was a three-and-a-half-hour drive mostly on Interstate 95, and it was largely unremarkable, except for uniquely named rest stops like Walt Whitman and Clara Barton that I used as benchmarks to gauge progress. It was typically a trip I made in my 1995 Mercury Sable—white with grey interior and bench seats—that used to belong to my Grandma Dottie before she passed. But on November 23, 2007, I drove the 250 miles from northern New Jersey to our nation's capital in a moving truck containing everything my father owned.

"I thought you reserved a cargo van," I muttered, looking anxiously into the side mirror as I made a right turn out of the U-Haul parking lot.

"I did. They only had the big trucks available," Dad responded, as if the bigger truck was an upgrade.

"I guess we'll have to make it work," I said from behind the wheel of the massive, twenty-six-foot vehicle.

I felt like I'd been making it work for years—maybe even my whole life. My father, my family, my childhood to that point had never truly lived up to my expectations. Too often did I fall into the trap of resentment, freeing myself through a combination of denial and distraction. That day was no exception. I pushed the power knob on the radio and hit the seek button repeatedly until 92.3 appeared on the display. Eddie Vetter's unmistakable voice came through the speakers in the front doors, belting out the lyrics to Pearl Jam's "Why Go" on K-ROCK.

A few minutes later, with my mom and brother in her silver Chevy Impala following behind, we arrived at my Aunt Eileen's condo where my father had been living for the last year or so. It was a plain-looking two-story row house in an unfinished senior living community in Somerset, New Jersey. Everywhere she went, Eileen leaned forward with a look of concern that I often interpreted as warmth until the moment she eventually said something that amounted to, "Hmm. Well, that's too bad." Most of the time, I didn't blame her for that attitude. She was a few years older than my dad and had landed there after a recent divorce. My father made the move with Eileen because he had been living in the basement of the house that belonged to Eileen's ex-husband.

Unfortunately, the situation was no longer tenable for her. Eileen was dealing with some of her own health issues, and the prospect of continuing to accept even minimal responsibility for my father was daunting. He needed increasingly more help to navigate his day-to-day routine given the steady progression of his condition, and Medicare wouldn't cover the cost of a home health aide or similar types of assistance. I also suspected Eileen was justifiably growing more and more weary of my father's signature crude humor and anxiety-inducing falls. I was grateful she had supported her brother for this long, but it was time for her to pass the torch to her nephew. I had begrudgingly and cautiously accepted.

I began steadily moving my father's stuff from his bedroom on the second floor down the stairs—a dangerous reality he was forced to reckon with—to the truck outside. The process was a bit surreal. On one hand, boxing up my father's personal effects was a deeply intimate act of support. It felt almost intrusive, unwillingly voyeuristic. On the other hand, I felt like I was helping move a friend and college roommate who had been transplanted from the 1980s.

So much of my dad's possessions were relics from the height of disco, perhaps a reminder of a time when he was happier, young, free, and full of energy. Atop a stack of VHS tapes, John Travolta gazed intensely from the cover of *Saturday Night Fever*. I put him into a translucent plastic bin along with dozens of loose cassettes, the likes of which included the Bee Gees, Michael Jackson, Kool & The Gang, and Earth, Wind & Fire. As I headed back to the stairs with another load, I passed by the abstract blue and yellow shapes of a vaguely familiar Joan Miró print leaning against the wall. A single crack ran across the glass from the left side of the frame to the right.

Consistent with my father's chronic disorganization, relatively few of his items were actually packed and ready to move. With help from my mother and brother, we worked steadily to fill boxes, duffel bags, suitcases, and whatever other containers we could find. My father had a particularly formidable collection of art supplies, amassed over the tenure of his career in the sign and display industry and then further expanded during his post-professional foray into drawing and painting.

While dad saw art as recreation, I saw it as therapy for his disease. It was an iterative practice that required focus and delicate repetitive movements, an activity that engaged both the body and mind. Whether recreation or therapy, or a combination of the two, art was incredibly valuable to my father since he could no longer work. And for that reason, I was happy to make half a dozen trips up and down the flight of stairs with markers, pastels, pencils, and acrylic paint. I was less happy to struggle with his forty-two-inch cathode ray tube television.

Even with help from my mother and brother, loading up the truck took just over two hours. It wasn't even noon, but it already felt like it had been a long day.

"Max, why don't you drive in the truck with your brother? I'll take Dad with me," my mother proposed.

"That's a great idea," I answered. I figured I would have as much time as I wanted with my dad in the future, so my mom could deal with him for the next few hours.

Lifting myself up into the cab of the truck, I turned to Max and asked, "You ready to do this?"

"Yup," he offered tersely, closing the door behind his six-foot, three-inch frame. It was about as much as I had come to expect from my younger brother. He was stoic in his expression and economical with his words. I always admired his ability to stay detached from the chaos around him, today especially. Meanwhile, I was feeling myself pulled gradually downward into a quicksand of doubt and uncertainty as we headed south toward Washington, DC.

Max slept for the majority of the trip, leaving me with the truck's radio and my own thoughts. I struggled to wrap my head around the implications of moving my father to DC and stepping into his primary support role. My mind was racing, trying to fast forward through time and achieve some kind of glimpse of what our future together would look like. It was no use, though. I remained restless but trapped in the driver's seat, my foot fixed to the gas pedal with a thousand pounds of my father's belongings behind me, pressing me forward at sixty-five miles per hour.

Every few minutes, my fingers would start to tingle until I remembered to loosen up on the wheel. I started to relax when I realized somewhere in Delaware that there was no turning around at this point. As much as I was terrified about what the future held, I somehow retained confidence that I would figure it out. I had a sense, though, that figuring it out would be a costly, emotional, messy, and frustrating process.

I backed into the loading area at St. Mary's Court as the sun was just beginning to dip behind the building across the street. My brother and I hopped down out of the truck to meet our parents at the entrance to the building. Glass enclosed a small carpeted lobby and the adjoining cafeteria area. A petite, older Black woman with thick-rimmed glasses greeted us and presented the key to my father's room from behind the front desk.

We rode the elevator to the third floor and headed a few yards down the narrow hallway. The door to room 308 revealed a three-hundred-square-foot efficiency, complete with a plastic accordion door that concealed the tiny stove, microwave, sink, and cabinets of the kitchen. The lone window in the room looked east over the building's small parking lot. The low-pile brown carpet stretched from one end of the small room to the other, giving way to a tight bathroom encased in green tile. It wasn't much, but it would do.

My brother and I worked methodically and silently to shuttle the furniture, appliances, bags, boxes, and bins from the truck to my dad's room. We unpacked a critical mass of items using the energy we had left, and then decided to call it a day just as evening approached. Among the final items I distributed across the room was my father's walker, which I set prominently near the door to his apartment as a not-so-subtle reminder of my expectation that he use it. Looking at my watch, I realized it was almost time for the daily dinner service at St. Mary's, and I wanted my father to have the chance to participate in his first meal with fellow residents.

After brief goodbyes, my brother and mother retreated to a hotel just around the corner for a one-night stay to get some rest before returning back to New Jersey early the next day. I left to head back to my apartment just a few blocks away, feeling intensely relieved that the move was complete and trying my best not to worry about the days and weeks ahead transitioning to this new reality. Still, I dreaded that it was going to be a brutal adjustment.

***

That evening, I had plans to grab dinner at a neighborhood bar with Brian, a friend and mentor from college. I knew Brian would be able to lend some perspective and allow me to vent, perhaps excessively. It was needed, and badly. As I was putting my coat on to head out, my cell phone buzzed.

"Hello, this is Josh," I said.

"Hi there, this is Mary Anne from the front desk at St. Mary's Court. Unfortunately, your father had a fall during dinner tonight," she said.

"Oh dear," I said, swallowing hard. "Is he okay?"

"Well, he tripped and landed on his head pretty badly. He cut his eyebrow open, and he was bleeding profusely," Mary Anne said.

"Where is he now?" I asked.

"He is over at the GW Hospital emergency room," she answered.

"I'll head over there now. Thank you," I said, masking my fear and embarrassment.

How could it be possible that my father had fallen already? It was only a couple of hours since I had left him. It was far too soon for him to have this serious of an accident. Even worse, falling during dinner on move-in day in front of everyone was on par with peeing your pants on the first day of middle school.

The GW Hospital ER was just a few minutes' walk from my apartment, so I was there in relatively no time. I checked in at the intake desk, and I was led back to the exam area. My father was already having his brow stitched up. He looked at me with shame from under the gloved hands of the doctor tending to his gash.

"Are you okay?" I asked.

"Yeah, I'm okay. I didn't see the leg of a chair sticking out," he explained.

"Were you using the walker?" I asked, eyebrows raised.

My father exhaled and looked away without answering. He didn't need to. The disappointment I felt in that moment was a sucker punch to the gut. I made a huge sacrifice in moving my father down to DC, and in return, I expected him to use a mobility assistance device to get around when outside of his apartment. It was something I had explicitly told him. It hadn't even been a day, and it was clear that he couldn't fulfill his end of the bargain.

"He's going to need a CT scan," the doctor said, tying off the last of the fifteen stitches in dad's head. "You can wait in the ER reception area."

I sat myself down in the waiting room and started fuming. I rehearsed the conversation I wanted to have with my father in my head a dozen times, but nothing seemed to soothe my anger. To make matters worse, I was dealing with a new emotion that might threaten me in ways I wasn't yet prepared for—bitterness. I didn't want to be dealing with this situation. It was unfair, and yet, it was a responsibility I had willingly decided to accept. I had to forge a way forward, and that meant managing my dad and managing my own emotions along the way.

An hour later, a physician's assistant in pale green scrubs brought my father out in a wheelchair. I helped Dad to his feet and supported his back while he established his balance. The first step was always the hardest, so I didn't rush him. He struggled to inch his feet forward, willing his legs to fire. After a moment, he began a normal stride toward the door slowly while I matched his pace, offering my hand if needed.

When we reached the sidewalk outside, I broke the silence. "What were you doing? I told you I need you to use the walker when you leave your room. At least use your cane," I pleaded.

"I know, I know," he said defensively.

"If this is going to work, I need you to meet me halfway."

He remained silent, looking forward and focusing on his steps. I attempted to walk closely enough to him to make sure he didn't fall on his face again, but just far enough away to let him think he was completely fine on his own. It was a new and strange balancing act I adopted almost unconsciously. I wanted to support him enough to maintain his forward motion, but no more than necessary so as to avoid bruising his ego.

I recognized the complexity in that moment immediately, though it was hard to fully wrap my mind around it. Our walk home together was one of those awkward dances we endure with loved ones who are suffering, an imperfect blending of hands-on intervention and hopeful observation. My father's willpower was clashing with the limitations of his physical body, and based on the stitches in his eyebrow, he was losing the battle. As his son, I needed to decide when to protect him from harm and when it was okay to let him fall. And I needed to learn to be okay with my decisions and the consequences that followed.

CHAPTER 3

OF CRAYONS AND CAMELOT

———

From an early age, most of us hold our parents to an incredibly high standard. We place them on a pedestal, and we hold tightly to the assertion that they are infallible. We assume, perhaps instinctively, that they know what they're doing at all times because they were the ones who brought us into this world. Our parents provide for us and nurture us, and we children innocently presume that honor, intent, and rationality guide each of their actions. Some children go as far as placing their parents in the "hero" category, elevating their standards and expectations that much higher.

But this is completely unrealistic. The more time I spent with my father, the more I realized he wasn't a hero. He was just human. He was doing what he could with what he was given, just like the rest of us. Unfortunately, he had been dealt a horrible hand, and he was playing it the best way he knew how.

Even in just a few months of serving as a caregiver to my dad, I was getting a taste of what it was like to be a parent.

Conversely, he was getting a taste of what it was like to take direction from his son. To that point, we hadn't been navigating the transitions well. Our interactions were messy and frustrating, and I regularly left his apartment feeling stressed and disempowered. I was disappointed in myself for not living up to my own expectation for the "parent" I wanted to be in those situations. The friction between my father and me could be explained, at least in part, by recognizing just how different we were. I was hoping that some of that friction could be soothed by acknowledging the ways in which we were somewhat similar.

My father was a very gifted artist. An eye for design gave him a creative edge running Associated Display, the sign-making business he took over from his father. I was lucky to inherit some of my dad's creative genes, and from early childhood, I took to art naturally. My father and I spent hours at the kitchen table drawing when I was a kid. He was fast and loose with his sketches, producing abstract figures and faces with the embellished features of a caricature. I was methodical and painstaking in my approach, doing my best to mirror reality on paper.

"What do you think?" He would flash me a smile as he held up his depiction of Bill Clinton speaking behind a podium, adapted from the front page of a newspaper atop the table beside us.

"That's him, alright," I said, having barely finished shaping a nose on my pad.

Perhaps our artistic styles reflected how we managed our belongings. Though some of my father's design talent rubbed off on me, when it came to keeping track of stuff, my father and I couldn't be more different. His organizing methods in his apartment at St. Mary's involved a series of mixed junk drawers while I kept my possessions more like supermarket inventory. Not so much as a toenail clipping had gone unaccounted for in my lifetime.

Not surprisingly, my father had an uncanny ability to lose and break items that most people find a way to keep and maintain for a reasonable length of time. He broke cell phones, for example, at an alarming rate. Sometimes I would find a way to recover them. More often, though, I'd be forced to replace them. Occasionally, the good grace of strangers would mean the difference between getting the old phone back and shelling out the cash for a new Nokia.

I was sitting at work one day, still fuming from the conversation I had with my father the night before about losing his phone. It bothered me to no end that he didn't seem to take care of his things. It worried me even more that it might not be because of his nature, but more as a result of his deteriorating dexterity and potential loss of cognitive ability. I'd like to think that if I were the one with Parkinson's, I would go out of my way to take *more* care when handling valuable, breakable objects. It upset me to think that his reaction to his physical decline might actually be to care *less*.

I found myself desperately clinging to the belief that my father was trying his best to be responsible for his phone, and that maybe he could realize just how much *I* cared about that.

When my phone vibrated in my pocket, I was surprised to see that the call was from my father's phone. *Hallelujah! The jerk found it*, I thought as I pushed the talk button. "Hey, Dad."

"Oh, hi there, am I speaking to Josh?" It was a voice I had never heard before. It sounded like a Black male in his mid-twenties. My dad was a Jew in his early-sixties.

"Yes, this is Josh."

"Uh, yeah, hi, my name is Ronnie, and I found this phone where I work as a line cook. I just called the most recent number to see if I could find out whose phone this is," he said.

It must be my lucky day, I thought. "It's my father's phone, thanks for calling me. He lost it yesterday. So, where do you work? Can I swing by and pick it up from you?"

"Sure, I'm working over at Camelot. My shift goes until 10 p.m. so you can come by before then," Ronnie told me.

"Ok, great. I'll call you back when I'm on my way," I said.

This was great news. Dad's phone had been found, and some generous Samaritan had paid it forward by returning it to its owner. I never liked buying a new phone for my dad since I was a student living on a tight budget, and I essentially played the enabler every time I procured a replacement. Camelot wasn't too far from campus, either.

As I put my phone back in my pocket, I did a double take as I remembered that Camelot was a strip club.

Despite being the self-described "home to Washington's finest show girls," Camelot was probably the last place I would want to venture in order to retrieve my father's cell phone. What was he doing at a gentleman's club? Did I even want to know the answer to that question? More importantly, how was I going to handle this conversation with him?

I squirmed uncomfortably in my desk chair. Sex was one of those topics my father and I never really discussed. It wasn't taboo as much as we both treated things as though we had already had a real conversation about sex, though in fact, I'd never had "the talk" with my dad. Instead, we just had a series of brief and incomplete interactions where sexuality and relationships tangentially came into view. Lest a pair of breasts flash across the screen during a movie we were watching together, I would stay perfectly still and silent until the scene was over, and neither of us would speak of it. Now, I would need to address the topic head on. And I was going to need to initiate and steer the dialogue, as if a guide forging the path through uncharted territory.

***

After my last class finished that night, I headed north from GW's School of Media and Public Affairs building to M Street. I called Ronnie about a half a block from Camelot, and just as I was nearing the windowless black facade, the heavy wood door of the club swung open revealing a tall, thin Black man in a red t-shirt and chef's apron holding a small gray Nokia. I shook Ronnie's hand, and looked him in the eye as I expressed my sincere thanks.

I turned from the strip club and headed in the direction of the assisted living facility, beginning a trip that likely hadn't been made before in history, that is, until my father came around. I turned the phone over in my hand as I rehearsed what I would say to my dad. Maybe I could just start by asking what he thought of the women? I knew little of my father's sexual preferences, but what tidbits I did know, I began reviewing in fine detail as I walked to his apartment.

When I was twelve, I discovered a stack of old Playboy magazines in my father's car. He must have realized I found them while I was taking a bit too long to retrieve something from his trunk, and he came to the front porch to yell, "Josh! Get out of there!"

My father was a flirt and a confident conversationalist who was never at a loss for words with women. He was shameless, and I could tell he took pleasure in getting a reaction from ladies anywhere and anytime. I had come to learn it was a source of tension in my parents' marriage. My mother was vocal in her disapproval, both to her friends and directly to my father, for his brazen fawning over women at the gym where he spent an inordinate amount of time.

I possessed very little knowledge of my father's partners other than my mother, but I did know that my mother was his second wife. My dad was married to a woman named Barbara for ten years, from the day he graduated college in 1968 until he was in his early thirties. After the divorce, I could only speculate about his conquests before my mother came into his life in the early 1980s. I had to believe that this period was when my dad hit "Peak Maury." He was newly single after a decade of commitment through his twenties, living in an apartment in New York City on 57th Street between 9th and 10th Avenue. By day he was working for his father at their sign shop in Hillside, New Jersey. By night, he was a regular at a roller disco in Chelsea called The Roxy. He loved to travel, too, often to singles resorts. If there was such a thing as a punch card for Club Med, my father would have had one.

In 1981, my father was on a flight from Newark to Fort Lauderdale to visit his grandmother. During boarding, as he approached his row with roller skates slung over his shoulder, he told a middle-aged couple that he had the window seat next to them. Their daughter, a pretty, young brunette chimed in from across the aisle without missing a beat. "Move over. Let him have the aisle seat." That was my mother. She was joining her parents, her sister, and a cousin to visit the new condo they'd just purchased a few weeks prior.

My mother and father chatted for the entire flight, and before leaving the plane, he asked for her phone number. When she got off the plane, my mother turned to her father. "I'm going to marry him," she said.

"That schmuck?" her father said. "No, you're not."

Two days later, my father took my mother out for their first date. They went to the beach, and after a short while, he suggested that they go roller skating in a nearby parking lot. Though my mother told him she liked to roller skate, she secretly hoped there wasn't a place to rent a pair of skates anywhere nearby. Luckily, there wasn't, and she sat down to watch my dad do his thing. My father laced up, hit play on his Sony Walkman, and proceeded to dance and spin and pirouette his way across the open asphalt wearing only a Speedo and knee-high sweat socks. Bare-chested and gleaming, he glided to music only he could hear, confident and carefree, as my mother and a small crowd of other admirers watched.

For my dad, everything was physical. My father had been spoiled by his good looks and a strong, muscular physique for most of his adult life. If it wasn't for the Parkinson's, I had no doubt he'd still be doing triathlons by day and club hopping by night. Clearly, it was a different story now. He wasn't operating out of his bachelor pad in Manhattan anymore.

His once six-foot, broad-shouldered frame was now hunched over, his biceps lean and his hair thinning and wiry. I can't imagine there was much drive left in him to pursue women, and even if there was, I doubt he was excited about the prospect of bringing anyone back to his room at St. Mary's. But had it come to this? I saw the strip club as a cop out for a man like my dad. A lack of ingenuity or imagination had brought him to a place where he was guaranteed a view, where a few dollars were exchanged for a manufactured jolt.

✳✳✳

A few minutes later, I took a deep breath as I knocked on my father's apartment door. Upon entering, as usual, I found his space cluttered and disorganized. A pile of t-shirts sat on the floor next to his hamper. Five colored pencils, all shades of red, were strewn across the carpet. An open box of corn flakes stood precariously near the edge of his small kitchen counter. After opening the door, Dad retreated toward his dark brown easy chair, shuffling his socked feet inch by inch without ever lifting them off the ground. He was clearly between doses of his medication.

"So…I have your phone," I said.

"Oh yeah? That's great," he replied.

"Yeah. A stranger found it, and he decided to return it," I explained. Simple enough.

"Great, where did he find it?" Dad asked me as I handed him back the phone.

"Well, he was one of the cooks at Camelot. I guess you left it there," I said.

"Ah, yeah," he said, with little to no shame in his tone.

"Can I ask what you were doing at a strip club? You're on a fixed income, right? I hope this isn't a frequent thing," I stated matter-of-factly, hoping to bring some objectivity to the discussion and inspiring his response to stay grounded in reason.

"I was sketching," he said.

"You were doing what?" I asked.

"They let me draw the women," he responded. "I come in with my pad and pencils, and I use the women as my models," he explained, as though it made more sense than anything in the world. To him, using topless dancers for nude models was just as natural as using a microwave to heat up a TV dinner.

"Oh, okay," I offered with all the coolness I could manage. The picture in my head was almost impossible to paint—an old man lumbering into a strip club with his walker and a tote bag full of drawing pads, charcoal, and markers.

"I don't feel comfortable going out to the art classes you signed me up for anymore," he added, opening up a bit further. "The ride on the Metro and the walk afterward are just a bit too much."

My dad was talking about a studio located in Alexandria he'd been attending for a few weeks. "I completely understand," I offered. That part made sense, but I was still in disbelief.

"Can you help me clean up a bit?" my father asked.

"Of course," I said as I collected a couple of half-opened pieces of mail from atop his comforter. I turned my gaze back to my dad, now straining to rise from his chair. Clearly he had moved on from the discussion, and I was shocked by how quickly he'd made the pivot. I wanted more of an explanation, but I could tell he wasn't interested in dwelling.

My head was spinning. I thought his explanation was bullshit. Was he actually drawing, or were the drawing supplies a way to get out of having to pay a cover and avoid tipping the entertainers? He didn't have the money to spend. He relied exclusively on a monthly Social Security check, the vast majority of which went to cover rent and the meal program at St. Mary's. What little expendable income my father possessed came directly from me in the form of "loans," though I wrote them off completely at the time I shelled out the cash. And most of that money was being used on art supplies, from what I could surmise.

Several thoughts flashed across my mind. Should I ask to see the drawings? Would that give me proof? Perhaps just intensify what was already a tense and awkward moment?

"Want to watch the Jets game this Sunday?" my father interrupted my inner monologue.

"Sure thing," I replied.

He was unintentionally signaling that he was ready to change the conversation completely. I gave him the pass on going further down this road.

My thoughts, however, were still on Camelot. And as I was rearranging the mess in my dad's apartment, it hit me. As much as I wanted to understand, I concluded that I wouldn't. It didn't matter how well I managed the conversation with my dad, whether it was tonight or any other night, whether it was heading to the strip club or anything else he'd done. Even if I asked all the right questions and got complete answers to all of them, I didn't know if any of it would have made sense. I didn't think I would ever understand why my father acted the way he did. His Walkman was playing a tune only he could hear.

And even if I could understand, I could do little to change his decisions. Though I often viewed him as the child in our relationship, I needed to remember that he was forty years my elder. He'd been through a lifetime more than I had, and he was experiencing the unimaginable weight of an incurable disease. He was motivated by things I couldn't comprehend, not because I wasn't capable of it, but because those things were far too complex to name and categorize into any kind of organizable taxonomy. I pondered the sheer hopelessness of my revelation, this impracticality of ever fully understanding my father and the impossibility of changing him.

As I let go of Camelot, I too let go of my aspirations of repairing my father. Letting go wasn't quitting as much as it was realizing that it wasn't the right goal in the first place. To build a meaningful connection to my father was to know him. And knowing my father was more about recognizing him for who he was rather than peeling back the layers to grasp the purpose of each of his actions. Camelot, and his reaction to me finding out about his trips there, was the embodiment of who he was: committed to his art, resourceful in the face of constraints, supremely confident, defiant of convention, and more interested in the Jets than explaining himself to his son.

I leaned over to pick up one of those red colored pencils off the ground. The shaft proclaimed it crimson. "Where do you want this one, Dad?"

CHAPTER 4

MINING TRUTHS

On December 19, 2008, I found myself in my father's apartment at St. Mary's completely alone. This was the first time I had been there by myself without him. The time was two in the afternoon, and the sun was shining over DC, but the space around me was draped in shadow. The little light that broke through the lone window in my father's efficiency apartment revealed the cluttered confines of his living space. His bed, perpetually unmade, barely held on to the dark blue blanket that was otherwise resting on the floor. A tower of mismatched, dirty plates and bowls teetered in the sink. His crowded desk was lined by piles of loose papers, a mix of his sketches torn from a pad, and what looked like medical bills. In the next forty-eight hours, I'd be required to remove everything from the room.

I'd moved my father to Washington a year ago, but I hadn't sorted through his stuff at the time. His things were encased in boxes and bins and stuffed in bags and suitcases, and the mission was solely about getting him to DC. Now, the task was different. I wasn't simply relocating my dad; I was moving him into a nursing home.

Just as the next stage of my father's journey represented a gross invasion of his personal existence, I would now need to dig into his personal effects. Logistically, there simply wasn't room to keep nearly any of it. His new living space was considerably smaller, and he shared a room with another resident. The real estate to which he now laid claim included a chest of drawers, a nightstand, and a small closet. I would need to be strategic about what he could retain and what would need to be disposed.

As I moved toward his desk, I felt like an intruder. I decided to start with the filing cabinet that I had placed there thirteen months ago, an item that looked as though it hadn't been used at all since it arrived. I inched open the top drawer to find it completely packed with paper—not filed but stacked vertically—and eventually pulled it out all the way. It looked like coffee had been spilled down one side of the misaligned pile, browning many of the sheets, which had crinkled since being doused. I pushed aside the chair and kicked away two shirts on the carpet to clear a space, grabbing the top half of the papers so I could begin to organize the mess while seated on the floor. As I knelt down, the faint mustiness of the room grew noticeably stronger.

Within the chaos, I discovered dozens and dozens of bills, each carrying past-due charges, and notices from debt collection agencies. There were pages and pages of discharge instructions from GW Hospital. That was really only the start, though, as the rest of what I found produced a potent mixture of curiosity, betrayal, disappointment, and anger deep within my gut.

I had found the following: a napkin that simply said "Shonté" above a phone number starting with a "202" area code; a printout displaying a complex grid to guide decisions in blackjack based on your hand, where each square advised to either hit, stand, double down, split, or surrender; a Post-it note with the name, number, and address of a hypnotherapist in Mountainside, New Jersey; a multi-page chain letter suggesting that the recipient can make $800,000 in weeks by following a few simple instructions; an advertisement ripped from a magazine offering "Italy at Leisure" over fourteen days from $3,539.

I found letters from a series of different lawyers regarding my father's involvement in multiple automobile accidents, along with a slew of automated letters from the New Jersey Motor Vehicle Commission, the most recent of which began with, "Your driving privilege has been suspended indefinitely."

Across a series of tax-related documents, I tallied almost $100,000 in money owed to the Internal Revenue Service. Along with a 1099 form dated 2004 that contained my name and social security number from a contract employer I didn't recognize—evidence that my father was collecting income using my identity.

I found a greeting card I had given my dad at least five years earlier for Father's Day. Flipping it open, the printed message inside said, "Dad, you've always taught me that life is an adventure in progress, that many small steps are just as good as one giant leap... that if you dare to begin, the rest will follow. Thanks for being a real-life inspiration." Below the text, I had hand-written, "Thanks for being my guide and my hero, a true inspiration, and a source of undying comical genius. Love, Josh."

I uncovered a letter from an older married couple who knew my father well. Written in February, earlier that year, the flowing script contained the following message:

You're fighting a nasty battle, but keep up your spirits. No, it's not fair, but as we get older we learn that, hey, life is not fair. It's great that your son is nearby. I always knew that these supports were priceless, but as I fight my own health battle, I've learned the lesson many times over.

After two hours of prying open my father's past, I needed to take a break. I slid backward and leaned up against the bed frame. I exhaled slowly, looking blankly at the pile of documents I had unearthed, avoiding the weighty task of processing the new information I had just discovered. Most people don't do this kind of thing until their parent dies. It is part of the mourning process. But my father was still alive.

How had I come to be in that moment?

Two weeks prior, my father had called me in a frenzy one night around 10 p.m.

"Josh, you've got to get over here quickly," he said with urgency in his voice.

"What's going on?" I asked, trying to find a quiet place for the conversation. I was at a holiday party for a student organization at the home of our faculty advisor.

"It's an emergency," he told me. "I've got ticks all over my body, and I need your help to get them off."

"What? You've got ticks on your body? Are you sure?" I asked with a measure of skepticism.

"Yes, they've infested my apartment," he explained. "Please get here as soon as you can and bring tweezers and insect bite cream with you."

Forty-five minutes later, following a stop at CVS, I arrived at my father's apartment. I opened his door to find him sitting on the floor beside his motorized wheelchair, looking disoriented and squinting at his forearm. I froze in place at the sight, momentarily transplanted back to the doorway of my grandfather's room at the nursing home where he lived for many years when I was a child. I remembered one particular visit when my father and I arrived to find his dad sitting on the ground, screaming for help, completely unaware of his surroundings or our presence. History was echoing before my eyes.

"What are you doing?" I asked.

"I have bugs crawling all over my arm, Josh." He glanced up at me through fearful eyes. "Come look at this."

I crouched beside him to get a better look. The bugs he was referring to were freckles, and he had a tweezer to his skin to try and gouge them out. The action had produced multiple small bloody gashes in his flesh, including one that he was continuing to poke at until I grabbed his hand.

"Dad, I don't see any bugs," I said. "I need you to calm down and take a deep breath."

He looked at me with sheer confusion. "I think they're under my skin," he continued.

"No. No they aren't. There aren't any bugs, Dad," I tried to explain. "I'm going to need you to trust me. Please just trust me on this."

It took another thirty minutes, but I managed to calm him down and get him cleaned and bandaged. Shortly after, I helped him into some pajamas and then into bed. I left the apartment just after midnight.

Three days later, I got a call from the front desk at St. Mary's telling me that Dad had been transported to the GW Hospital emergency room. His hallucinations had intensified, and he continued to try and dig out the non-existent insects from beneath his skin. That day, my father had used the tweezers to pick at the skin just below his eyes. A concerned fellow resident notified the staff at St. Mary's and suggested that they check on him.

Late that evening, my father was admitted to the hospital. Following blood work, a CT scan, and a spinal tap, the attending physician told me that my father was exhibiting delirium related to his Parkinson's disease. Delirium was an unfortunate progression in his condition, a new layer of his neurological decline that would affect his cognition atop the growing physical impediments. I was told that my father would need to remain in the hospital to get a sense of just how severe his situation was.

The next few days revealed how far my father had drifted from reality. During each of my daily visits to room 405, he presented a new interpretation of the world around him through the prism of his delirium. He demanded that I bring him antibacterial soap for bugs that were still crawling in his beard. He insisted that I prevent the press from coming into his room. He claimed that he exposed himself on television, and that the police were coming for him. He asked why people were being kept in a cage in the hallway. He thought I was an Israeli assassin coming for him.

Early one morning around five thirty, I got a call from the hospital telling me they needed to put my father in restraints because he was trying to leave his room. When I visited later that day, during a fanciful rant, he became eerily quiet for a few seconds before breaking the silence. "Josh, I think I might be dying," he said, looking me right in the eye. "Promise you won't leave me."

Throughout it all, I was an impotent witness to the spectacle. Of the many physicians I spoke with, one of them told me that my father had Lewy Body Dementia, an umbrella term that refers to the buildup of protein deposits in the brain that affects thinking, behavior, and movement. Another told me that my father had twelve months to live, and the drugs he was on might make that quicker.

After my father had been at the hospital for a week, I had a conversation with Margaret, the Executive Director of St. Mary's Court.

"I'm going to recommend that we move Maury into nursing," she suggested.

"Okay," I replied, nodding, without any disagreement in my tone.

"But honestly, it's less of a recommendation. I can't allow him to come back here," she said.

"Got it. So really, there's no choice for me to make. Is there?"

"Yes, that's right," she said. I could sense the genuine compassion in her voice. "Feel free to blame me. But I know you agree with this," she said. "He needs much more support than St. Mary's can offer."

The last year had been rough. There had been dozens of falls, starting with the night I moved him into the building. He once fell while shopping at Radio Shack, toppling a display of batteries and dislocating his shoulder in the process. At one point, he fell walking into his apartment and flipped over during his descent to the floor, producing a four-inch laceration on the back of his head. His trips to the emergency room were often painful in and of themselves. He would sit, sometimes for hours, waiting to be seen while his medication wore off. By the time he was evaluated, he was completely immobilized with rigidity and was barely able to speak, which made the diagnostic and treatment process significantly more complex.

During one of these incidents, I came to the GW Hospital emergency room to track down my dad and was able to locate him by the sounds of his strained moaning. When I reached his room, he was completely still but wincing with his eyes shut tightly. A catheter line was running from under his gown to a bag filled with yellow liquid at the side of the bed.

"He told us he desperately needed to urinate, but he wasn't able to get to the bathroom, even with help," the resident explained. I squirmed with vicarious discomfort after hearing the explanation.

Most of the trips and falls happened during the evening, when the medicine was starting to taper, and as a result, these ER visits would sometimes conclude well after midnight. It scared me to consider that these were only the incidents I knew about. There were likely countless more that didn't require immediate medical attention but were nonetheless serious.

After nine days, my father was stable enough to be discharged from GW Hospital. He had responded well to Seroquel, an anti-psychotic, which helped manage his delirium. During moments of clarity, I had attempted to explain the situation to Dad, and his reaction made things that much tougher.

"I can't believe it's come to this," he reflected. "I've turned into a little old man. Most people die within two years after moving into a nursing home."

From the hospital, he was transported to the Washington Center for Aging Services (WCAS), a public long-term care facility run by the District of Columbia. Though I would have preferred to tour and vet at least a handful of nursing homes, WCAS was the only one that could immediately accept a male Medicaid patient. As such, there was no choice yet again.

Life moves quickly at the edges, those fleeting moments moving from the current to the next. Though I knew it was inevitable, this transition was happening sooner and faster than I ever thought it would.

My mind came back to my father's room as I realized my fingers were still wrapped around a stapled packet of papers. I gazed down at the official-looking document. "Fair Oaks Hospital Discharge Summary, June 22, 1990," was typed in plain Courier font across the top. The document was a detailed description of my father's three-week stay at a residential psychiatric facility in Summit, New Jersey. I was five-and-a-half years old at the time, and my little brother had been born ten weeks prior. The chief complaint said simply, "I am here for depression. I want to feel better." Among an extensive medical and psychosocial background narrative, I came across a line that I believed to be true nearly two decades later: "Patient reported a good relationship with oldest son."

PART II

CHAPTER 5

DESTINATION TRANSFORMED

DC summers are well-known for their heat and humidity—so much humidity you wring the air out into a bucket. Despite my love of warm weather and spending time outside, there were days on which the conditions were simply too oppressive to enjoy any outdoor activity. In August of 2009, we were having a seasonable summer, and I dedicated one particularly warm Sunday to spending time with my father.

A few months prior, I had moved him into the Hebrew Home of Greater Washington, a senior care facility in Rockville, just outside of DC. To get there, I took the H2 bus from where I was living in Mount Pleasant to Cleveland Park, and then rode the Metro out to the White Flint station. After leaving the station, I walked the fifteen minutes to the Hebrew Home campus in the steamy, eighty-seven-degree weather, feeling hot and damp as I approached the entry to the Wasserman Building. The sliding doors parted, rewarding me with the chill of perfectly conditioned seventy-degree air. The muted sounds of cockatiels chirping reached my ear from their cage at the far end of the lobby. I glanced in their direction to see the usual row of residents in wheelchairs lined up facing the floor-to-ceiling window, silently squinting through sunlight out into the parking lot before them. I signed in at the front desk and received my white, oval sticker with the word "visitor" above the Hebrew Home logo.

I walked through to the elevator just past the lobby and hit the call button. After what felt like five minutes, the doors opened and I shuffled in. "Can you hold the elevator, please?" A pajama-clad resident rolled into view, rhythmically rocking his wheelchair forward a few inches at a time. His wheels got stuck in the small gap between the floor and the elevator car. I waited, initially frozen out of courtesy, trying to mind my own business and let him regain forward inertia. After a moment, he looked at me as if to say, "Are you just going to stand there?" I quickly helped him get his chair inside the elevator and hit the button for the fifth floor.

When the elevator opened, I stepped out and reached for a pump of wall-mounted hand sanitizer. The faint smell of disinfectant just barely covered a combination of body odor and urine. I turned the corner to see Elinor, the yenta of the fifth floor, awaiting my arrival. A few thick white hairs protruded from her chin and pink slippers covered her feet. "Your father's doing great!" she reported eagerly. She didn't allow me to finish saying, "Thank you," before continuing on with a combination of unintelligible garble punctuated by oddly personal questions about my dating life. After a couple minutes, I managed to peel myself away.

I rounded the nurses' station and pulled up to my father's room, slowing my pace as I reached his doorway. His room was compact but serviceable, and I'd worked diligently to maximize the use of floor space given what we had squeezed into his quarters. To my left was a folding door to a private half bathroom covered in shiny blue tile and bathed in bright white fluorescent light. A mirror cabinet enclosed my father's toiletries, which I restocked with regular frequency. A hamper rested at the foot of his fully adjustable bed, under which I had slid a series of shallow plastic storage bins containing art supplies. A large sitting chair encased in maroon faux leather sat awkwardly in the corner, as ugly as it was uncomfortable. A small nightstand doubled as a desk for my father's computer, and behind it I had shoved a cable box, router, and a nest of perpetually tangled cords. A chest of drawers contained the sweatpants, pajamas, and t-shirts that made up my father's daily ensembles, above which stood a forty-inch flatscreen TV projecting the Mets and Dodgers at Shea. On my right, a closet contained jackets, blankets, and extra pillows behind two white sliding doors. The walls were covered with a mixture of photos of family and friends and some of my father's artwork, along with the same hideous floral wallpaper that adorned the hallways. My father sat at the edge of his mattress, in the middle of it all, leaning over his walker. He turned his head toward me and smiled as he realized I had arrived.

"What would you like to do today, Dad?"

"How about a movie?" he quickly suggested.

Two weeks prior, the Hebrew Home had arranged for a trip to the movies for residents, and my father had loved it. He enjoyed every minute he spent outside of the building. Who could blame him? He lived at a sleepaway camp that never ended, except some of his fellow campers couldn't remember their own names and he got in trouble for trying to do too much on his own.

"I took the Metro here," I replied. "I don't have a car, so I can't drive us."

"We don't need a car," he explained. My father's response was so nonchalant that I didn't hesitate to accept it as unequivocal fact. "When we went to the movies a few weeks ago, the drive was only five minutes."

"Alright, let's do it." I didn't mind walking as long as my father was medicated, I thought.

Within a few minutes, we were getting ready to leave the Hebrew Home. I had asked the nurse on duty for an extra Sinemet, which I often did for multi-hour excursions, which would keep dad as "in control" as possible while we were out. The medication prevented him from experiencing stiffness and rigidity throughout his body. During his "off" periods between doses, he was pretty much locked in place, and walking would be difficult and painful, at best. His speech became little more than a breathy whisper, where words came out in a stutter or were slurred together as if he were drunk. The off times gave me respect for my father's medication. Thinking about what a small chunk of man-made chemicals could do was incredible.

With the help of his walker, my father made his way out of his room and toward the elevator. He had taken a dose of medicine about an hour before, so he was in good shape as we left the building. "The theater is just a bit north on Rockville Pike," he explained as we turned right out of the Hebrew Home parking lot and took the sidewalk on Montrose Road. Just a bit north sounded good to me.

It seemed hotter outside than when I arrived at the building. I was already sticking to my t-shirt and we'd only walked a few hundred feet. We made our way on sidewalks and cut through a strip mall parking lot to meet up with Rockville

Pike. At one point, we followed a parking lot around a big box store on speculation that it might be a short cut. Unfortunately, there was no outlet on the far side of the store, and we had to backtrack several hundred yards. I could swear the sun grew angrier as we retraced our steps. A blue Toyota Camry slowly drove by us, and I looked on with jealousy.

By the time we reached Rockville Pike, we had already been walking for thirty minutes. There was a gas station on the corner, and Dad asked if we could stop for a Diet Coke. I went into the tiny convenience shop and opened up the refrigerator. I took an extra second reaching for the bottle, wiping the sweat from my forehead.

"Do you want to sit down?" I asked my father when I got back outside, cracking open the twenty-ounce bottle for him.

"No. Let's keep going." Despite the heat, he remained locked on our destination. He pointed his walker back toward the sidewalk, and we began moving steadily once again.

At that point, I began to doubt the whole operation. I realized that this was the first time I had ever gone to the movies without knowing what was playing, without choosing a movie to see, and without having chosen a time to see said movie. The unknown was unsettling. I wasn't in control. Time was usually the best leverage I had against my father in situations where I needed to leave him and start living my life again. This was one of the first times I'd made a promise to spend time with him and I hadn't thought at all about what I might be getting myself into. I realized that this was a mistake.

We plodded on. I had no way of calculating the distance to go, no knowledge of the area, no map to gauge the relative location, no smartphone to route our path. This outing was so uncharacteristic of me: the consummate planner, the to-do list builder, the agenda crafter. I had trusted my father, who never planned much of anything in his life, and that was a bad decision.

We walked mostly in silence, though I made attempts to prompt discussion every few minutes to check in and gauge his mood. My father wasn't very talkative, and he'd been pretty quiet since we left the nursing home, which was a good thing for me since I wasn't in the mood for conversation. We were an hour into the walk, and still no movie theater in sight.

I knew, looking at my watch, that the time was rapidly approaching when my father's medication would stop working. It's often difficult to judge when the pills would wear off and when it made sense to provide him his next dose. As a result, timing his meds was an artform. I knew for sure that in this instance, we really wanted to limit the lag time between the effectiveness of the current dose and the moment his next pill would kick in. During that period, I knew he wasn't going to be able to walk.

"I'm starting to lose it, Josh." My father was barely audible, and I could tell he was straining to form the words. He was hunched further over his walker than he had been just a few minutes ago.

"Let's take a rest," I offered, trying to exhale the frustration building within me over what was easily a mile and a half. "There's some shade just ahead."

The stretch of road and sidewalk we'd traveled, mostly along Rockville Pike, was completely devoid of benches, so I helped Dad fold down the leather padded seat on his walker and engaged the brakes. I positioned one hand in his armpit and another on his back and helped lower him into the cushion.

Without hesitating, I reached into my pocket and offered him the extra Sinemet pill. Rummaging through the tote bag that was haphazardly tied to his walker and filled with a few dozen colored pencils and crayons, I pulled out the Diet Coke I'd bought for him earlier at the gas station. The Diet Coke was two-thirds gone, and what remained was maybe a few degrees cooler than the sweltering air. I held the tiny blue pill up to his mouth and popped it between his lips. I raised the bottle up to his mouth and tilted it toward him. Dad gave me a subtle nod and I lowered the Coke. There was little of the soupy drink left, and it looked like half of it was easily my father's backwash.

"So what do you think here?" I asked, my head slightly cocked to the side, eyebrows raised and hands on my hips.

"I think we're close," he responded.

Oh really? I thought. Unfortunately, I had little information at hand to either confirm or deny his projection. "Alright. You got it." I hoped he could sense the sarcasm in my voice. "You ready to keep going?"

My father looked at me, remaining quiet for a few seconds. His silence was all the response I needed.

"Maybe I can push you for a little while?" The words came out before I knew what I was suggesting.

"Sounds good. Let's try it," he said.

I think my naiveté got the best of me because I didn't even know if the walker could function as a wheelchair. I figured I would give it a shot. I disengaged the brakes and began pushing my father down the sidewalk.

The wheels of the contraption were small and made of hard rubber. My father's shoulders vibrated as the walker rumbled over the rough concrete. Each crack between the sidewalk was like a reverse speed bump—a speed dip—that forced him to perform a sudden, involuntary nod. Albeit a rather bootleg means of conveyance, the walker appeared to be up to the task, and my father was able to remain fixed in the seat as I pushed.

I could sense that we'd be tested as we approached our first intersection. The intersection was a small one-way road leading up to a merge with Rockville Pike. There was a yield sign for the traffic attempting to access the Pike and a striped pedestrian crossing. A minivan was approaching the intersection, but it was slowing, and I made eye contact with the driver. One nice benefit to walking with my father anywhere was that drivers and pedestrians alike were incredibly courteous.

I approached the curb cut in the sidewalk with caution but also a dash of confidence. I figured the best way to navigate the sidewalk-to-blacktop transition was to keep momentum. Unfortunately, my reasoning was flawed. I didn't see it, but the asphalt was an inch higher than the bottom of the curb cut. The four-inch wheels on Dad's rollator were ill-equipped to handle the transition, and the downward slope of the sidewalk was setting us up for a high-speed collision with the edge of the pavement.

From the instant when the front wheels struck the blacktop, time slowed down, as if to force me to endure the events that followed in hours rather than seconds. It seemed as if we'd hit a short, invisible wall. My father and the walker both tilted forward and upward instantly, rotating above the front wheels. I crashed into my father's back, adding to his momentum. Recognizing what was happening, I leaned my shoulders over his head and threw my hips backward to counteract the forward movement. My entire body was lifted off the ground with the upward force of the walker.

Adrenaline surged as I feared my dad would fall face first into the roadway, my body crushing him as I followed.

I desperately lifted my right leg backward, straight out, trying to slow our momentum. We came to a point where we were nearly balanced on the walker's front two wheels, paused halfway between salvation and disaster. My father was leaning forward at a near forty-five-degree angle, and me on top of him, now hopelessly flailing my entire body to prevent catastrophe. Miraculously, the momentum reversed and we slowly descended, the rear wheels touching down on the sidewalk with a mechanical thud.

The driver waiting for us to cross must have initially been wrapped with fear, but then shortly after wept with joy, having borne witness to the tragic comedy we just put on. Though I didn't glance over, I wanted to think he was sitting mouth agape behind the wheel, beginning a slow clap as we regained our footing. I just wish he could have taken video of the whole incident so I could see if from his perspective.

I think this event kicked my father back into gear, or maybe it accelerated the rate that the medication spread into his bloodstream. Perhaps, he was scared I might inadvertently dump him out of his walker onto the street again. Regardless, he was ready to start walking again on his own. I helped him out of the walker, now with all four wheels on the ground, and we were back on our way.

Another thirty minutes had gone by before I saw a landmark I recognized, the Rockville Metro station. I asked a stranger near the station where the movie theater was, and he pointed us in the right direction. The walk was short from there to the Regal 13. In this case, short actually meant three minutes.

We crossed the blazing hot parking lot, amidst tens of cars, as I reflected on the notion of convenience as a virtue for the weak. Making our way to the ticket window, I looked at the movie choices. None of them were particularly appealing: an animated movie about monsters in which I had absolutely zero interest; an action flick full of blood and gore, judging from a trailer I'd seen online; an adolescent comedy that was sure to be chock-full of penis jokes. The only reasonable choice was *Transformers*, the Michael Bay shoot 'em up, blow 'em up sci-fi robot adventure. The only problem was that it didn't start for another thirty minutes. Given that we'd already come this far, what was another half-hour? Plus, I was hungry, and there was a burrito place next door. "Let's get some food while we wait," I said.

After a quick meal, we headed back to the theater. I wasn't particularly impressed by the movie, but Dad really enjoyed it. "It's amazing what they can do with computer-generated effects these days," he ruminated.

Almost six hours had passed since we left the Hebrew Home. I looked out at a blue-orange sky as I held the door for my father to leave the theater. I had taken for granted the air conditioning I'd been sitting in for two and a half hours; despite the setting sun, the parking lot felt like a sauna.

I could tell my father was stiffer than usual. His meds were running out again, and this time, I had nothing in my pocket better than lint to offer him. I had taken a gamble by giving him the backup pill earlier, knowing he'd potentially be worse later on. "Why don't we take the Metro?" I suggested.

"I think that's a good idea." He smiled at me.

Our walk to the Rockville station was slow and careful, and the subsequent train ride was predictably quiet and, thankfully, uneventful. We got off at the White Flint station, two stops later, where I'd arrived earlier that day to visit my father.

Walking from that station back to the nursing home with Dad was strange. I had taken that path alone so many times, and now he was taking it with me. I felt a tinge of resentment for him—that walk was mine and mine alone. I owned that stretch of parking lot and sidewalk between the White Flint Metro Station and the Hebrew Home. I've told those trees, bushes, cars, and stores all about my frustration and helplessness. This path was my space, a deeply personal space, and it provided a critical therapeutic function. This walk was a portal from my world to his, a buffer zone that aided in the transition. I didn't realize how uncomfortable it would be to have him make that walk with me. It forced me to share a stretch of the world that I had gotten so used to experiencing by myself.

We made it back to my father's room after what seemed like days. He had missed dinner, so the nursing staff had brought a meal to his room on a tray. I navigated Dad to his bed and took a peek under the maroon-colored plastic cover atop the plate. I found mashed potatoes with gravy and Bubbe's baked chicken, a staple at the Hebrew Home and one of my father's least favorites. Admittedly, it didn't look very appetizing.

"Alright, Dad, I've gotta take off," I said, commencing my farewell ritual. I set him up at the table in front of the food and gave him a kiss on his forehead.

I left the facility and took a seat on the bench outside. I was drained. My shirt was damp with sweat. I stared blankly ahead for a few seconds, trying to piece my thoughts together. Later I would map the route and discover that we walked three miles to get to the theater from the Hebrew home, and luckily, only about a mile and a half to get home, thanks to the Metro.

Still seated, I looked toward the entrance to the building where a resident in a wheelchair was taking a long drag on a cigarette. Her curly hair was partially matted to her forehead, and one of her wrists was in a rigid plastic cast. Our glances met, and I raised my eyebrows and pulled my mouth to the side as if to humbly say, "I just don't know." She was unfazed and continued to stare at me, unblinking.

I had an English teacher in eighth grade who recognized me for someone with too tight of a grip on the steering wheel, always bent on finishing the drive as soon as possible. Back then, Mrs. Knapp gave me a piece of advice I'd thought about often but hadn't really understood until that day. At middle school graduation, she handed me a card that ended with the line, "Remember to enjoy the journey, not just getting there."

Caring for my father simply couldn't be about the destination. What if it *was* just about the destination? What was the destination for him? Was I simply ushering him toward death? All the while keeping him in the safe and predictable confines of the nursing home he so viscerally resisted? Instantly, I became "cool" with walking four miles with my dad while he struggled, at times, to put one foot in front of the other. I was fine with going to the movie theater without knowing what was showing or when we'd get there. I was okay with not having somewhere to be at that very instant.

Suddenly, that wooden bench outside the nursing home was comfortable, like I had just sunk into a well-worn couch in a close friend's television room. I couldn't remember the last time I sat still, enjoying where I was, with no thought of where I was headed next. I drew a full breath of warm, wet air and exhaled deeply.

CHAPTER 6

THE DRILL...

On the afternoon of February 18, 2010, I was listening to *Contra*, Vampire Weekend's second album, waiting for my afternoon coffee to hit and carry me through the end of the work day. My phone buzzed, and a 202 number popped up on the screen.

"Hi, this is Leslie from the neurological surgery department at The George Washington University Hospital. Is this Joshua?"

"Yes, speaking," I replied.

"I'm calling to follow up on your father's consultation for deep brain stimulation. Is Mr. Lasky still interested in moving forward with the procedure?" Leslie asked plainly, as if it were an annual cleaning at the dentist or a physical exam by a family doctor.

A year earlier, I had taken my father for the consultation. Deep Brain Stimulation (DBS) required a complex surgery to implant a pair of electrodes in the left and right sides of the brain, each wired to a battery pack implanted in the chest. The battery pack worked like an electrical pacemaker, sending a specified voltage to the electrodes, which were positioned in proximity to dopamine-producing neurons.

The theory was that the electrical impulses stimulated the production of dopamine—which my father lacked because of his Parkinson's Disease—and thus, alleviate several of his symptoms.

"Yes, I believe so," I said.

My father had been interested in the procedure for a long time, even before the FDA approved it. He'd heard about the success that doctors in Europe had seen with their patients, and he knew his condition was only getting worse. Since the consultation, Dad had brought up the surgery on occasion. I was always supportive of moving ahead, but I wanted to make sure he had the time to let the idea incubate, to consider the consequences, to weigh the potential benefits and risks. I had not remembered that during our consultation nearly eleven months ago, the doctor had "penciled in" a date for the surgery one year in advance.

"Does the date still work for him?" Leslie asked.

I froze for a minute to think. My father was about to have a pair of holes bored into his skull, and I didn't want to commit him until he was ready. Or at least as ready as he'd ever be. "I'm going to have to check with my father. Can I call you back later?"

I ended the call and dialed my father. I explained the situation to him and put the question out there for him to consider. "What do you think, Dad?"

"Well, it's very soon," he said. "But do I really want to wait any longer?"

"That's sort of the way I look at it. Plus, it's not like you'll have months to revisit the decision and stress out," I offered, trying to sound optimistic. "The lead up time will be quick and painless."

"Yeah, maybe for you!" His reply made me smile.

That Saturday, I brought my father to GW Hospital to have a pre-DBS CT scan, which was required in advance of the surgery. I was told that the images produced would enable doctors to pinpoint the locations that would receive the electrodes. It seemed like such an inexact science, but I had no choice but to retain faith in the experts that were about to cut into my father's head in one week's time.

After the visit to the hospital, I brought my Dad down to the National Mall. Though I had graduated (twice, no less), I went to practice with the GW Ultimate Frisbee team in East Potomac Park that afternoon. My father had seen me play only a handful of times, which I thought was a shame, especially for someone who had spent innumerable Saturdays at traveling soccer team games watching his uncoordinated elementary school-age son play kick-and-chase. I was much better at ultimate than I ever was at soccer. While a freshman at GW, my father had come to an ultimate tournament I played in at Rutgers University in New Jersey, and Dad sketched a picture of my team in a huddle that I promptly framed and hung on my wall. As a senior, I had co-captained the team and, since graduating, had tried to mentor some of the younger players who were now assuming leadership roles. One after another, members of the team introduced themselves to my father. Barring his association to me, the disheveled, shrunken old man hunched over his walker could have easily passed for a person experiencing homelessness. I was overjoyed that he could meet the team and to have him there, back on the sidelines watching me, even though it was just a practice.

This type of occurrence was rare. Far too often did I compartmentalize my life such that time with my father was completely separate from time with friends. Admittedly, the opportunities to have my father present when I was hanging out with friends were few and far between, but I often felt as though I was living two lives. One life was the early-twenties young adult trying to build a career during the week and running around town getting drunk with his friends on the weekends. The other was a much older, jaded adult figuring out how to care for an ailing father. I savored those moments when I could lead one life, where my entire world was contained within my field of vision, if only for the sense of calm it provided.

In the days that followed, I planned out the logistics of the day of the surgery. My father needed to be at the hospital at seven thirty in the morning on Thursday, March 11. Accounting for the forty-minute trip from the nursing home to downtown DC, plus time on each end to park and get my father in and out of the car, I would need to be at the Hebrew Home no later than a quarter past six. I also needed a car. I got in touch with my father's cousin Jeff, who lived in Bethesda about fifteen minutes from the nursing home. A regular visitor to see my father and a genuinely kind soul, Jeff immediately offered to let me spend the night in his guest room and borrow his car for the day.

On the evening of the tenth, I made my way out to the Friendship Heights Metro station where Jeff's wife Elinor picked me up. She brought me back to the house and showed me to their guest room. The room was a cozy, dimly lit space lined with shelves that displayed framed pictures of the family, including Jeff and Elinor's daughters and grandchildren.

I was prepared not to sleep at all that night, so the two hours that I eventually got were like a bonus. I was incredibly anxious and uneasy. For hours, I ruminated on a series of unanswerable questions that had flowed through my consciousness over the course of the previous two and a half years. These were prompted by the flashes of a scene playing out in my head in which a doctor was telling me that my father didn't make it. I was unable to gauge my reaction to the hypothetical, and it stirred doubt deep within me. I resolved to be confident in my decision to support my father having the procedure, if only it meant that we were taking a calculated risk in exchange for a richer quality of life. Arriving at that place of understanding, I was finally able to get some rest.

The shrill of my cell phone alarm woke me from what was essentially a glorified nap. I retrieved my father in a state of half-sleep, and we sat in silence during the drive from the Hebrew Home to GW Hospital. I found a good parking spot near the hospital entrance and we were surprisingly on time. At the surgery check-in, I sat my father down and went to speak to a nurse. After scribbling his information onto a sign-in sheet, I was handed a small packet of papers. It contained a pamphlet about GW Hospital, FAQs for surgical inpatients, and a yellow form of several pages titled, "Making Your Medical Choices Known."

"Does your father have an advanced directive?" the woman behind the small counter asked.

"No, he doesn't," I responded, swallowing nervously.

"You may want to have that discussion with him," she suggested.

"Okay. Thank you," I said, knowing it was definitely not a discussion I wanted to have with my dad. That was also not the time I wanted to be having it. I walked extra slowly back to the seat next to my father.

"You're all set," I said. "They'll call you when they're ready to take you to pre-op." Without thinking, I pulled the yellow form from the bottom of the pile of papers in my hands and put it on top.

"What's that?" my father asked, looking at the stack of papers in my lap.

"Well, they asked me if you had an advanced directive, and I said no." My heart was suddenly thumping in my ears.

"Oh." I recognized the look in my father's eyes at that moment. I had seen it a few times before. The look was a rare instant where he was forced to acknowledge his own mortality. "I guess we have to discuss that, huh?"

"They suggest that we fill it out. I know you don't want to be doing this now, but I think we should."

After a very short deliberation, my father concluded that he wanted the instructions to simply read, "My son Joshua Lasky will make all decisions regarding my health in the event that I am unable to do so myself." I wrote out the statement, and Dad signed with his crooked right hand.

Twenty minutes later, we were called into the pre-operation area. The area was a large hall that had been divided by hanging curtains to split the room into several small rooms, each with its own hospital bed. My father was ushered to an open bed on the opposite side of the room, where we were told to wait. Another twenty minutes passed before we were greeted by the two doctors who would be working together to complete the procedure. These two men would be using power tools to install electrical wires in my father's brain.

Though the doctors were calm and soothing, it was incredibly painful to watch what happened next. The surgery required a kind of vise to be fitted around Dad's head to hold it in place while the two holes were bored through his skull. One of the doctors injected a local anesthetic in four places on my father's scalp, points at which the vise would be secured. Each of these injections produced a swollen mound of flesh, from which blood oozed as the vise's screws dug into his skull. It looked extremely uncomfortable, but my father retained his composure. The surgeons circled around my dad, making fine adjustments to the contraption, tightening one screw and loosening another, and repeating the process until things were perfect. Finally, one of them announced, "Alright, I think we're ready."

I gave his hand a squeeze and looked him in the eye. "You're tough," I told him. "You can do this. I'll be waiting for you." Dad exhaled a deep breath and gave me a half-smile. I smiled back and headed for the waiting room, thinking, *I sure as hell hope this works out.*

CHAPTER 7

...AND THE SHOVEL

Roughly eight hours later, at two thirty, my father's surgeon appeared at the end of the row of chairs in which I was sitting. I turned to him as he took a seat next to me.

"Your father's in recovery now," he said. "The surgery went well. Preliminary results were positive. Your father exhibited increased mobility and flexibility when impulses were sent to the electrodes."

"That's great to hear," I said, exhaling with relief.

"You'll need to wait until the battery pack is calibrated in a few weeks by the neurologist before you start making fine-tune adjustments to the settings," he continued. "But this is a step in the right direction."

I followed the doctor back to the recovery area where I found my father kicking his legs beneath the sheets and shaking his gauze-wrapped head dramatically from side to side. He was moaning unintelligibly as a nurse attempted futilely to get his attention.

"Dad, it's me, Josh," I said with the most soothing voice I could, approaching him and resting my hand on his left shoulder.

"Oh, Josh, thank goodness," he said, his darting eyes decelerating their movement and eventually resting on my face. "You've got to get me out of here. I don't know what's going on, but I think they are trying to drug me."

"They are trying to drug you, but it's okay," I told him. "You just had your surgery and it went really well. You need to take some medicine now for the pain, okay?"

"Okay, okay," he said. His breathing started to slow, and his legs came to a rest under the sheets.

The nurse shot me a quick smile and continued with the process of setting up the intravenous sedative.

"Try to get some rest. Okay, Dad?"

He gave me a nod and blinked a few times. Then he closed his eyes. "Okay," he said.

Later that afternoon, my father was transported from recovery up to room 449. The medication in his system meant that he spent the rest of that day and that evening sleeping or in a sleep-like state. At eight o'clock that night, I visited his room to find him snoring. I gave his hand a gentle squeeze before turning to head back to the car and go home. It had been a long day, and I was looking forward to getting some rest.

Twelve hours later, following a full night's sleep, I returned to room 449. To my shock, the room was empty. I backpedaled out of the door and turned to the nurses' station across the hall.

"Hi, I'm looking for my father, Maury Lasky. Where is he?" I asked, a sharp edge in my voice.

"Your father had a seizure last night. He was moved to room 580 in the ICU," she responded matter-of-factly.

"What? He's in the ICU?" I blurted. "Why didn't I receive a phone call?"

Before letting her answer, I had turned and taken two steps in the direction of the elevator bank.

A minute later, I was at the ICU waiting room, picking up the phone and asking to be admitted through the entrance. A buzzer sounded, and I pulled on the brushed nickel handle of the heavy door.

I found my father lying in his bed at the center of a sprawling, day-lit room. His face was covered by an oxygen mask, and his wrists were secured by restraints. I stood at the entrance to the room, fixating on the condensation that appeared and disappeared with each of my father's exhalations. I was startled when a young resident in a long white coat with her hair tied back came up behind me.

"Are you Mr. Lasky's son?"

I learned that my father's seizure last night was likely caused by a small amount of air inside the brain cavity. Luckily, none of his vital organs were affected, and a CT scan didn't reveal any serious problems in his brain. He was in restraints because he kept trying to remove his oxygen, whether or not he was doing so intentionally. Unfortunately, I wasn't provided a real explanation for my father's state of semi-consciousness, just that it could take some time for him to wake up. I was also told that my father would soon need to have a feeding tube put in to provide him with medication.

"If you see him start to convulse, push this button," the resident said. "We've got him on Ativan, so he should be okay."

I found my way to the blue armchair at the far end of the room next to the window. I worried that I had done this to my father. That I was responsible. That the pressure I put on my dad to have the procedure had led us to this moment where he lay comatose, somewhere between asleep and dead.

I involuntarily crossed my arms and leaned forward, shrinking in the chair.

That afternoon, a trio of doctors appeared, and they let me know they needed to insert a tube into my father's throat. One of them produced a device that looked like a pickaxe with a shortened handle. The device was a laryngoscope, a probe designed specifically for the purpose of intubating patients. They leaned over my father's upper body and began the procedure. I turned away, unable to bring myself to watch. After ten seconds passed, I heard my father coughing, and I got the sense that there was an issue. After another ten seconds, I noticed a slight look of frustration on the faces of the doctors attempting to place the tube. My father began gagging and choking violently as the scope and accompanying tube pressed downward into his throat. After a full minute, the doctors paused their efforts. They explained that Dad's altered anatomy—a likely result of his severely hunched posture—was creating an unusual level of difficulty. Several attempts later, as the sounds of horrifying gasps and gurgles filled the room, the tube was placed into my father's esophagus. Something, however, wasn't right, and my father was unable to breathe with the tube in his throat. The doctors quickly removed it, and my father immediately took a long breath.

At seven thirty that night, while leaving the hospital in complete emotional disarray, I got a call from the admissions office at the Hebrew Home. They told me that their policy dictated that my father's bed would be held for only fifteen days. After that, we'd need to reapply for residency at the facility. At a moment when I was hoping to start cleaning out my wounds from the events of the day, it was as if someone had just covered them with a handful of dirt.

Two days later, instead of showing signs of waking up, my father had become more somnolent, which was presenting a problem. He needed nutrition and oral medication, and to this point, the doctors had been unable to confirm that the now inserted nasogastric tube had been properly placed due to my father's altered anatomy. They brought in an x-ray machine which confirmed that the tube had in fact not been inserted correctly. A gastrointestinal specialist was brought in to attempt to place the tube, but this proved to be unsuccessful also. Though it was not a preferred option, my father needed to be sedated so that an endoscope could be used to insert the nasogastric tube, along with a breathing tube. He was already in state of semi-consciousness without sedatives, and there was a worry that placing him on a breathing machine would create a dependency that would be difficult to remove.

Returning from a trip to the cafeteria on the ground floor, I came back to my father's room to find him breathing very awkwardly, as if sucking on air, his head tilted back, and his eyes wide open. He had dried blood in his nostrils, and his lips were severely chapped. I ran out of the room to call the nurse as I heard him choking with each breath. The nurse on duty motioned to a doctor just down the hallway and they rushed to my father.

"Your father's tongue was blocking his airway, but it's cleared now," the doctor informed me. "Unfortunately, we can't wait any longer, and we're going to need to intubate your father at this point."

An hour later, my father had been placed on a ventilator, and the nasogastric tube had been properly inserted. I couldn't really tell whether he was improving or not, whether we were moving forward, backward, or sidestepping. The best my twenty-five-year-old mind could do was attempt to make sense of the explanations I was given by the professionals who swarmed around my father all day, every day. I found it laughably frustrating that the neurology and neurosurgery teams had, at times, completely conflicting opinions of how my father had come to be in his current state and what was needed to bring him back to solid footing. My job as an advocate was made even more difficult by the fact that I was painfully and woefully alone. I spent dozens of hours sitting silently in that blue chair beside my father, studying the shapes and sounds of room 580. The machines standing vigil over my father chirped in sequence. The muted thud of sneakers pattered over linoleum tile. A ball point pen scratched paper on a plastic clipboard.

Over the next few days, my father seemed to become more responsive. Occasionally, he would gently squeeze my hand when I spoke to him. I got the sense that there was marginal improvement. Unfortunately, this was coupled by a fever, and after some tests, it was confirmed that he had pneumonia, which added to the stress on his respiratory system. Layered on top of that, my father was producing a lot of fluid excretions that needed to be routinely cleared by the nursing staff. Despite their continuous stewardship, he was still left with a thick orange crust that coated his tongue between cleanings.

My father's condition became a seesaw of tradeoffs: more sedation brought more pain relief, but it also limited his ability to clear the secretions from his lungs; more time on the ventilator meant continued risk of infection and pneumonia. After a week in the ICU, my father experienced a "desaturation" event in which his oxygen levels dipped dangerously low. I was asked to provide authorization for the placement of a percutaneous endoscopic gastrostomy tube, a feeding tube to be inserted surgically through the wall of my father's abdomen and into his stomach.

After approving the procedure, I stepped outside into the crisp March air. I sat on a concrete bench in the plaza adjacent to the hospital, at the entrance to the Foggy Bottom Metro Station. I called my mother to give her an update as I gazed lifelessly at the green visitor wristband next to my Casio watch.

"Why are you keeping him alive, Josh?" she asked me. "You're prolonging his suffering."

I hadn't shed a tear to that point, but at that moment, I began to cry uncontrollably. I allowed the frustration and the sadness to envelop me fully as I watched the strangers pass by on the sidewalk in front of me. Five floors above, my father was suffering, but my work as his advocate in that moment wasn't about choosing to end or prolong his pain.

Regaining my composure, I explained what I had heard directly from the doctors. "Deciding not to put in the stomach line would have been to actively decide to starve him," I said. "It wasn't really a decision at all."

After I hung up, I found myself thinking back to an easier time, a time before decisions were even real. I thought back to carefree Saturdays in the summer during my childhood. My father would get up early and head to the shop for a few hours to make sure his staff was on pace to complete fabrication for their latest job. Just as I was tired of watching cartoons, the screen door would smack against its frame, and I'd hear the jingle of a key chain clipped to a belt loop. My father would appear with a brown bag full of turkey sandwiches from Mr. Sub on Kenilworth Boulevard.

Not long after, we'd be heading south on the Parkway to exit 100B. We would park as close as we could to Second

Avenue Beach and make our way to a spot on the sand next to the families we had come to call our "Bradley Beach crew." I would go boogie boarding with my little brother and build castles at the edge of the water. My father would take me on runs, and we'd play paddle ball or throw frisbee. At some point in the afternoons, he would break out the shovel—not a plastic toy shovel, but a real contractor's shovel—and dig a giant hole for Max, our friends, and me to play in.

As the sun lowered in the sky and the shadows became longer, I would wish time to slow down. I'd wish to keep us there on the shore, tucked against the tumbling waves, our skin golden and our lips smiling and salty. I would reach down for a fist full of sand and try to keep the warmth in my palms as I felt the grains slide down between my fingers.

The weeks that followed Dad's surgery were a mix of small ups and downs, seeing incremental progress followed by incremental decline. Overall, however, there was net improvement in my father's condition. He was removed from the ventilator and transferred out of the ICU to a stroke recovery floor. He slowly gained greater consciousness, though he became wildly agitated at times. My father was given Seroquel to manage his hallucinations, but they persisted doggedly. One evening, I came to visit my father and discovered him in a fitful rage, completely naked, writhing in bed. He had pulled out his PICC line and was bleeding over the sheets. He scratched and clawed at the feeding tube entering the left side of his torso as I made my way to the side of his bed while calling for help.

After weeks, I had burned through all of my vacation and sick hours, and I began working from my laptop in the corner of my father's hospital room. I watched over him while he slept, and when he was awake, I got up from the computer to stand by his side. We had short conversations while he was lucid, and then he would descend into confused obscurity.

"I'm being held captive against my will."

"They're keeping me here so they can butcher me. Aren't they?"

"At least take me out of here for Passover. You can get me some matzoh ball soup."

"The government is great. Isn't it?"

My father's second cousin, Mark, came to visit the hospital, finding my father in a state of semi-consciousness but breathing loudly and laboring to pull air into his lungs. Mark looked at me with shock, suggesting with his eyes that we needed to get help. I explained, perhaps too casually, that a nurse had just been here, and that there was nothing we could do to help him breathe easier.

With tears in his eyes, Mark turned to me and said, "I have the utmost respect for what you are doing for your father."

On the 29th day at GW Hospital, my father was finally discharged. He was transported to the Hebrew Home, where he had a new room on a different floor. All of his belongings had been boxed up and stored during his month-long absence. I broke open the cardboard to find a stack of t-shirts wrapped in plastic, unworn since their last wash in the facility's laundry room. I pulled out a framed photo of my brother in Argentina drinking yerba mate next to a campfire, and I placed it atop the dresser.

Both of us exhausted, I helped my father from his wheelchair and positioned him in bed.

"It's a good thing you're strong," he told me.

CHAPTER 8

SILENCING ALARMS

The months following my father's deep brain stimulation surgery and extended hospital stay were challenging for him and me both. Any benefits offered by the procedure were overshadowed by the trauma to his brain and his body from four weeks in the hospital, including those two weeks in intensive care and the eight days on a ventilator during which he battled pneumonia and fought for his life. Like scars from war, both the PICC line in his arm and the percutaneous endoscopic gastrostomy in his stomach remained in place for weeks.

My father underwent extensive physical, occupational, and speech therapy, engaging in a dozen or more sessions per week on the ground floor of the Hebrew Home. I struggled to see meaningful progress, though I acknowledged the therapy as something to keep him engaged. My father was largely unable to regain enough control of his hands to continue making art, and his inability to create left him without one of his most important venues to escape. His voice became weaker and weaker, and his words started to blend together into an indistinguishable blur. When he was between doses of Sinemet, I would have to tell him to yell after attempting to discern what sounded like an inarticulate whisper.

The surgery must have tripped a circuit in my father's brain that caused his behavior to shift significantly. A few months after returning back to the Hebrew Home, I got a call from the social worker assigned to the residents on my father's unit.

"Josh, I'm sorry to have to bring this up with you," she began, as serious as I had ever heard her over the phone. "Your father asked one of the nursing staff if she would have sex with him."

"Oh my," I said in disbelief. "Is it possible that he was joking?" I asked, curious and hopeful that maybe this was a misunderstanding.

"No, he wasn't," she answered quickly. "We don't provide that here," she explained, as if the clarification was needed.

As if that wasn't bad enough, I began to notice more paranoia and delusional thinking creeping its way into our daily conversations. My father concocted stories about mistreatment by the staff that were simply too farfetched to be true. In the fall of that same year, he experienced episodes of extreme agitation, which would start with a refusal to take his medication and then evolve into verbal and physical altercations with the nurses trying to help him. During a particularly extreme episode one night, he needed to be restrained by two nurses but still managed to bang his head against the wall until it started bleeding. Shortly after, he was transported to Suburban Hospital for evaluation and treatment, though he was discharged without being admitted. I visited a few days later, pleading with my father to calm down, to no avail.

"The nurses ripped me out of bed and pushed me to the ground," he claimed. "They dragged me through the hallways. They put an injection in my fingers, and I was allergic to it."

"I don't think they did that," I said, attempting to soothe him.

"They took me to a motel, and then they turned up the juice to a machine and zapped me," he explained. "I think it was a car battery."

"You have to trust me, Dad," I told him. "These people are here to take care of you."

"Josh, I've trusted you this long, and look where it's gotten me."

Witnessing this was painful. During this prolonged period of cognitive and emotional instability, I gained a new appreciation for the power of mental illness and its ability to warp my father's reality into a fatalistic nightmare, often with little to no warning. We were in the middle of a conversation about my latest project at work when my father pulled out a plastic bin of his sketches and started to place each piece of art in the trash, one by one.

"Don't do that, Dad," I told him, a look of concern on my face.

"Don't worry, you can have them," he said dryly. "I'll be dead soon."

A few minutes later, he calmed down and started asking me if I saw anything good on the television channel guide, as if everything was fine.

"Can you order that movie where the guy takes a pill that makes him smarter, stronger, and more appealing to women?"

"*Limitless*?" I suggested. "Sure, let's watch it."

Thankfully, over the coming weeks, my father gradually returned to a more stable ground through a series of adjustments to his medications, which now included anti-psychotics and anti-depressants. And though my father's physical condition continued to decline, the fight within him was as powerful as ever. One night, I got a call from Wanda, the charge nurse on duty.

"Your father left the facility without permission," she told me over the phone.

"What? Where is he?" I asked, confused.

"He's here now," she said. "But he had gotten all the way to Rockville Pike, and he was found by the police. They brought him back."

"Okay, good to hear," I replied with relief..

"I recommend that we think about moving him to a locked unit," she said.

Though my father wasn't moved to a locked unit, his wheelchair was outfitted with an alarm, pleasantly called a "wander guard," to prevent him from leaving the floor. A proximity sensor would activate the alarm if he rolled past a certain point in the hallway. The device doubled as a deterrent for my father to stand up out of the wheelchair as well. It was fitted with a string that clipped to his shirt, and if the base of the string was pulled out of its port, the alarm would sound.

The wander guard was also connected to a proximity sensor near the elevator bank. While on my visits, when my father and I would arrive at the elevators, the alarm would begin blaring and I would have to quickly hit the buttons on the numeric keypad to make them stop. My fingers moved involuntarily to the sound, a muscle memory response to the painfully shrill beep. I had punched the code in so many times I didn't even know the numbers, just their relative position on the keypad. I couldn't imagine how many times my father had tripped these various alarms without me there, and it hurt to think how long he might have to endure their ear-piercing declarations before one of the nurses was able to hush them.

At times, my father proved himself to be both creative and resilient despite his physical limitations. His "whatever-it-takes" attitude was both inspiring and appalling, as I learned during a visit when I picked up a lone sneaker in the middle of his room. His shoe was damp and reeked of urine, but I only realized it after the shoe was in my hand. According to my father, he had fallen out of bed the night before at two in the morning and was completely unable to get up. His call button was out of reach, so he yelled for the nurses. After an hour of shouting for help, he felt the urge to pee. He couldn't get up to get to the bathroom, but his black Fila tennis sneaker was just within reach, and it was temporarily repurposed as a urinal. After hearing the story, I immediately dropped the shoe and headed for the sink to wash my hands.

Throughout, my father remained desperate to get out of the Hebrew Home and I worked diligently to oblige. Whenever possible, I borrowed or rented a car so I could take him away for a few hours, usually to somewhere just a few minutes down the road but an entire world away.

On a Sunday in February of 2012, I was pulling into the Hebrew Home parking lot after a shopping trip to Target. I had rented a Mazda 3 through Zipcar, and we were getting close to the time I would have to return the vehicle to its parking space outside the Twinbrook Metro Station. Looking to my father in the passenger seat, I could tell he was in good spirits. For him, attitude was essential. He was in a good place emotionally, and his body language showed it. His speech was clearer and his movement more fluid because of it. I contrasted it with moments when I'd seen him upset, during which he tended to be much slower, stiffer, and harder to understand. That, in turn, made him even more depressed. In that moment, I was excited to see a smile on his face and hear the energy in his voice.

Sunday afternoon was a popular visiting time at the Hebrew Home, and upon quick inspection, I didn't see any open parking spaces within a hundred yards of the entrance. I pulled the car up to the roundabout at the main door and unloaded my father's wheelchair from the trunk of the car. I left the car in that spot with the hazards on and returned my father to the sitting area on the fifth floor adjacent to a few other residents before heading back down to the car a few minutes later.

"Hey, asshole," I heard a voice nearby call at me. I turned to face a man in his mid-forties standing next to a blue Volvo station wagon just behind my rental. "You can't park here."

Before I could raise my eyebrows in dismay, the man dropped into his car and closed the door. I watched, mouth slightly ajar, as he pulled away with his wife checking her makeup in the visor mirror and his two kids playing with each other in the back seat. *If he had any idea*, I thought.

As the weather warmed up that spring, I began to ride my bike out to see my father with greater frequency, and it quickly became my preferred way to get out to Rockville. There was something special about riding my bike. Sure, I didn't have to navigate the parking lot and deal with other visitors who felt it was their duty to tell me I was breaking the rules, but it was much more. The ride provided important time and space for me to meditate, to reflect, and to breathe. Riding my bike was a practice that helped center myself as I prepared to see my dad, not really knowing what to expect, and to reflect on our latest set of interactions after the fact. The ride was also a way for me to reconnect with my body. I spent a lot of time in my own head, and I relished in both the physical dimension of riding combined with sensory immersion of the world passing by at ten, fifteen, or twenty miles per hour.

Late one Thursday evening at the end of March, I left the Hebrew Home after a particularly difficult visit with my dad. He had been insistent that I bring him to a different neurologist than the one we had been seeing for years. Although I had told him I would make the call the next day, he said he couldn't wait. I had needed to step into the hallway right away to pretend I was making the phone call. I was exhausted from the visit, but I was looking forward to getting back on my bike.

I rolled out of the parking lot and headed east toward Rockville Pike. I turned right on Nicholson Lane then made a quick left on Woodglen Drive, riding past the Whole Foods and leaving the glow of streetlights for the darkness of the Bethesda Trolley Trail. A much more pleasant strip of pavement, the trail was a straight, tree-lined path completely deserted at that hour. The waxing moon barely reached its rays through the still-bare trees and my bike light had run out of battery. As a result, I was forced to rely on the residual glow of distant streetlamps and outdoor lights on houses fifty and a hundred feet away to help me make out the edges of the pavement. The skin of my nose, cheeks, and forehead was cold against the winter air, but the rest of my body was burning as I pedaled vigorously to shorten the distance between myself and my apartment. I was going at the only speed I knew how to go—as fast as I could—knowing twelve miles still lay ahead of me.

I wove my way on the twisty path around the National Institutes of Health campus and into downtown Bethesda, stopping at a red light right before I transitioned onto the Capital Crescent Trail. I saw a couple leaving a restaurant on Elm Street who were glancing down the road with anticipation for the next available taxi. Two friends walked quickly toward the entrance to Bethesda Row Cinema as chilled breath fanned out from their faces. The light turned green and I turned the crank, standing up out of the saddle and quickly getting back up to top speed. The street became a sidewalk, and the sidewalk became a dark, tree-lined paved trail once again.

Eight miles left to go. I looked up at the moon, a crescent tilted at forty-five degrees. I smiled back, considering whether to add a few miles to the ride home. A new sense of liberation and peace washed over me.

CHAPTER 9

BEYOND THE
BREAKING POINT

With the starting horn, I leapt forward shoulder-to-shoulder with a hundred others, the soles of our sneakers producing a muted hum as we covered the grass. The narrow course was lined by the same bright orange plastic netting you might see at the end of a construction project, and we were being corralled toward the first of a series of more than thirty obstacles and physical challenges. Glancing to my right, I found an opening in the pack leading toward the edge of the group. I shortened my stride and veered through a half dozen other runners so that I was within an arm's length of the course boundary and then turned up my pace to head to the front of the field. This was the elite heat of the ten-mile Super Spartan, and even though I had never run an obstacle course race before, I was dead-set on competing for a spot on the podium.

Two years prior, on a Saturday morning, my friend Andy and I showed up to a beginner parkour class at a gym converted from an old fire house off of New York Avenue in northeast DC. We were both desperately hungover, and somehow, I managed to avoid being sick during two hours of jumping, crawling, balancing, and climbing. However, Andy wasn't as lucky. That ended up being his last appearance at Primal Fitness, but it was my first of hundreds. I took quickly to parkour as I enjoyed the combination of strength training, movement, and finesse. It also seemed to follow logically from my obsession with fringe athletic hobbies, which started with competitive Dance Dance Revolution in high school and continued with ultimate frisbee in college.

Combined with my natural running ability and a baseline of cardio fitness, my parkour skill set would, in theory, make me a force to be reckoned with at the obstacle course race. I was confident as I pulled up alongside the runners leading the race, easily matching the seven-minute per mile pace. We turned a corner and I saw the first obstacle, a six-foot plywood wall. Without slowing down, I jumped and landed my right foot against the wall while grabbing the top edge with both my hands. In one swift and smooth motion, I pulled my hips up above the wall, gently planting my left foot on the top of the wall and letting my momentum carry me forward and downward. I reached for the ground with outstretched legs and absorbed the impact, bending my knees and moving directly into a forward roll before popping up to standing a half-second later and instantly speeding back up to full pace. I glanced over my shoulder to see that I was three seconds ahead of the other runners just starting to crest the wall.

Fifty more yards of grass led to the second obstacle, a four-foot wall raised about two feet off the ground. I could either hop over it or crawl underneath it. I remembered that my sneakers had been wet even before I started running, and there was an ample amount of dew on the grass as a result of the unseasonably chilly August morning. I sped up as I came within a few feet of the raised wall and dropped down to the ground into a baseball slide, leaning slightly on my right hip and tucking my right ankle under my left knee. With hardly any friction, I glided easily under the wall and used my hands to push myself back up to standing. I was feeling confident, and at that point, about ten seconds ahead of the other runners.

Leading a race is exhilarating, but it's also nerve-racking, especially since this was a first for me. The course was painfully obvious, so I wasn't worried about losing my way. However, I had to believe that the obstacles were going to become intensely more difficult. To make it worse, I didn't have the luxury of seeing other runners' strategies for tackling the walls, ropes, crawls, monkey bars, and whatever else was coming. When I had asked, the only piece of intel about the course I was able to get from a race official was, "You will get wet."

After a short uphill section, the course leveled out and I spotted the next obstacle. The obstacle was a raised platform that dropped off into a pool of water four feet below. *There's the water,* I thought. Without hesitation, I ran up an incline that led to the platform, took two steps, and then launched off the edge from my right foot. I flew forward and began my descent to the surface of the water, expecting to be fully submerged shortly after. But as my left foot touched the top of the water, it almost instantly collided with the ground below it, and I heard an audible "crack" that echoed in my ears. Momentarily disoriented, I kept striding forward out of the much-shallower-than-expected pool and toward a trail that entered a forest and meandered uphill through the trees.

Suddenly and without warning, immense pain began emanating from my ankle, reverberating through my body each time my left foot made contact with the earth. I took a few quick and deep breaths and leaned into the incline. In my head, I was telling myself, "I think I might have sprained it, but I should be able to finish the race." The pain pulsed from my lower leg, hot and blinding, but I was committed to pushing myself forward. I took a dozen more grueling steps and realized I was slowing down involuntarily. Within a matter of seconds, the lead pack had caught up to me and passed effortlessly. Something was horribly wrong, and my body was resisting every effort I was making to will it up the hill. That's when I decided to look down at my leg. My left ankle was the size of a grapefruit.

I was instantly filled with dread and regret. I wanted so badly to unsee that sight. I wanted so badly to go back to that ledge and prepare for a gentler landing. I wanted so badly to go back to the starting line and run a slower, more cautious race. It didn't matter though. The pain of my reality was so deeply unavoidable that I needed to get myself off the course and to medical help. I slowed down to a hobble as I spotted an aid station some one hundred yards away through the trees. Blood was throbbing loudly in my ears, making the sound of the leaves crunching under my feet sound distant. I limped slowly at first and then staggered as I realized my left foot simply could not take any weight. If I tried to walk on it, I would collapse. I hopped my way the last fifty yards to the tent where I finally found relief in a plastic folding chair.

Ten-minutes later, I was in an ambulance headed to Inova Hospital in Leesburg, Virginia. My gurney was wheeled into a large exam room where I had an x-ray and then was told to wait with my leg propped up by a couple of pillows.

"Well, it looks like you broke your fibula," an emergency room doctor declared as she entered the room. "Unfortunately, I think you'll need to have surgery."

I was speechless. I had never broken a bone before, so I didn't know what to expect. I didn't have the words to react. After a moment, I regained my focus. "What's the timeline for getting back on my feet?"

"Hard to say right now. You'll need to talk to a surgeon as soon as possible," she explained. "It's probably at least four months until you're walking again, and at least six before you should think about running."

The words were devastating. My mind was reeling trying to comprehend what the future would look like. Since I was a child, I had never been good at sitting. I was always in motion, running, playing, hiking, or riding my bike somewhere. Stillness had never appealed to me. There was always somewhere to go and something to go do. Though I had never truly acknowledged it, movement was an important part of my identity. Movement was essential to my being. Movement was life. How depressing that I finally acknowledged it in that moment with my fractured leg sticking up in the air. I felt utter despair and bewilderment in my newfound immobility. This wasn't me. This couldn't be me.

Presenting a pair of crutches she produced from a closet at the far end of the room, the doctor asked, "Do you know how to use these?"

***

Twenty-four hours later, I was being wheeled into an operating room at Georgetown University Hospital. I was anxious and worried. I had never had surgery before, and this was the first of two procedures required to repair my busted fibula. Initially, the doctors would need to install a titanium plate secured by seven screws along with one longer screw that pinned my fibula to my tibia. The second surgery was to remove that longer screw once my torn ligaments had healed. The plate and seven screws securing it were intended to stay with me for the rest of my life.

As I looked upward from my rolling gurney, the drop-ceiling tiles and fluorescent bulbs of the hallway gave way to powerful spotlight beams in the operating theater. I was told to count backward from ten. I got as far as eight before begrudgingly letting go and succumbing to the anesthesia.

Instantaneously, I was somewhere else, surrounded by pale blue curtains suspended from the ceiling. The recovery room air was filled with the staccato of faint beeps coming from all directions. I pulled the sheet away to see my leg heavily bandaged from the kneecap down. I closed my eyes and tried my best to take deep breaths.

That night, and the nights of the next several weeks were terrible. Not only was I in severe pain, but I was deep in anguish. I was full of rage at the world and my inability to process and accept the destruction I had unintentionally wrought upon my body. I was fixated on what I had lost because of the accident, and I tossed and turned wrestling with regret and self-pity. The little sleep I did get was perforated by the throbbing in my ankle, prompting me to reach again and again for the Vicodin. The discomfort was like barbed wire, latching on to me and digging in with sharp barbs each time I tried desperately to push it away.

I was frustrated by my suddenly eroded independence. I needed crutches to move more than a few feet, I required extra time to wrap up my cast in plastic bags before showering, and

I had to ask for help getting groceries. Accessing my third-floor apartment was instantly intimidating, and climbing the forty-two stairs to reach my door was a painfully slow process. The "click-bump-thud" of my ascent quickly became a depressing anthem for the routine. I placed both crutches gripped by a single hand on the step ahead of me, grabbed firmly onto the wooden railing, and hopped my right leg up to the step where I had placed my crutches.

The founder of parkour, Georges Hébert, a French physical educator, is credited with saying, "Etre fort pour être utile." In English, "Be strong to be useful." I felt neither, and instead I sank deeper and deeper into a static despondence.

In the darkest moments, I stumbled upon a devastating speculation that prompted waves of stress to wash over my body: that I might one day become my father. I knew in my head it was irrational, but emotionally, I couldn't help but indulge in the conjecture. As his progeny, we shared so much in common: our mannerisms, our humor, our looks, our athleticism. Being injured was life-altering for me, but I knew I would eventually heal. But a Parkinson's diagnosis was a one-way trip. The disease was life-defining for my father. I hated the notion that I, too, might be faced with a future like his. I hated even more that I was so ill-equipped to deal with even a temporary limitation like a broken ankle. I had half my leg confined to a cast for a few months. If that was hard, how would I fare when my entire body breaks, when I become mere consciousness trapped within a human form, as my father had essentially become.

My visits to see my dad during this time were logistically difficult and emotionally painful. I couldn't reasonably stop at a pharmacy or pick up food or bring him clothes because it was hard enough dragging myself out to Rockville to see him. I didn't feel comfortable letting him use a walker while I was on the crutches, and I couldn't push him in his wheelchair. My negative attitude enveloped me like my cast, and it colored my interactions with my father. He didn't empathize with me one bit during that period. He knew I wasn't happy, but I couldn't tell whether he was choosing not to engage me on the topic of the injury, or if he just wasn't sympathetic. He had every right to think I was whiny and bitter.

After twelve weeks, my cast was removed. Something about that moment helped me turn a corner both physically and psychologically. Perhaps there was a metaphor for that instant, but I didn't feel much like a butterfly emerging from its cocoon. My leg had withered in the cast, my muscles atrophied from lack of use. It was an ugly and discouraging sight. But the piece of me that had been imprisoned was now free. Though I wasn't back at the place from which I started, I could at least see a path to become strong, and useful, once again.

My second surgery went as planned, and then I began physical therapy shortly after. Over the coming months, I visited a doctor three times a week who specialized in sports injuries and working with athletes. I stretched and flexed dutifully to achieve more and more mobility in my ankle. Strength came back through tedious repetition. The doctor would dump dozens of marbles out on the floor and I'd put them back in a bucket one at a time using only my toes. The sessions were painful and monotonous at first, but I eventually saw the exercises as small but significant steppingstones. Over time, I started putting weight on the ankle, and eventually, I was able to walk. I moved from a position of self-pity to self-reassurance. I slept better at night and I started to look forward to each new day.

By early spring, I began to emerge from a months-long fog of doubt and despair. My wallowing had been winnowed, replaced by an optimism about the future. Against the backdrop of the misery and pain of the last several months came a new emotion I hadn't truly known to that point—gratitude. I had not appreciated my mobility, my strength, and my independence until they were taken away. I was earning them back, and I vowed not to waste them once I had them again. I owed that to myself, and I owed that to my father.

During this period, I vowed to stop taking my good health for granted, and I started brainstorming ways to push my physical limits. I needed to show appreciation for the capabilities I had that my father no longer possessed. I also needed to perform a reset on my life socially and professionally. Shortly after the accident, my girlfriend of two years broke up with me, and after months of feeling like I screwed it up, I focused on moving on. Toying with the idea of becoming a lawyer, I had spent the winter preparing for the LSAT, and though I sat for the exam in early spring, I ultimately decided against applying to law school. I had formed an LLC with the ambition of starting my own consulting practice, having become sadly disillusioned with my role as sustainability manager at the University of the District of Columbia, a gig I once revered as my dream job.

I recognized that I was in a state of tremendous transition, though none of the potential directions I saw for myself were all that inspiring. I felt a sense of potential brewing, but still felt stuck. In response, I spent weeks thinking about the things that made me happy and the things I had always wanted to do. One day in April, sitting in the bedroom of that third-floor apartment, I looked over at the map of the United States of America hanging from my wall. That's when the idea entered my mind, and I knew it was exactly what I needed.

"I'm going to ride my bike across the country."

CHAPTER 10

THE TUNNEL

On Sunday, June 16, 2013—Father's Day—I was sitting in my dad's room at the Hebrew Home, flipping my way through a shoebox of family photos: my Aunt Barbara, dressed in an eighties-style black bodysuit and a gold chain belt posing by the pool in her backyard next to Tango, her pet terrier; my father in a bright red, silver, and blue ski suit sitting with a beer after a day on the slopes in the Swiss Alps; my grandmother Florence smiling for the camera, wearing turquoise earrings and a pink blouse with shoulder pads too big for her tiny frame. It was a pleasant distraction as I was mentally preparing for a difficult conversation. I had procrastinated badly but needed to break the news to my dad that I'd soon be gone for three months.

I pulled an old black and white photo out of the box and placed it in my father's gnarled hand. He tilted his head and studied it closely through his glasses as they slid ever so slightly down the bridge of his nose. The image contained a young Sol Lasky and his business partner, both standing in front a massive sign that read "Zenith," one of their biggest clients.

My father chuckled at the image as he straightened up a bit in his wheelchair, though still comically slumped over. He was wearing a red Polo shirt, coated in spots with some unidentifiable remnants of lunch, and half his collar was standing up. He had a set of green plastic Mardi Gras beads around his neck that were handed out at a folk concert put on for Hebrew Home residents earlier that afternoon. "Did you know that my father never finished high school?" he said.

"No, I had no idea," I said, genuinely surprised. I waited to hear more, but nothing came. Looking at my father, I could see he wasn't interested in sharing. Though there was some joy in the memory of his father, I sensed that those memories were mostly of pain.

It had taken me almost four years of serving as a caregiver for my dad to gain a new appreciation for the importance of caring for myself. Since my earliest experiences on planes, I had never understood why parents were told to put on their oxygen mask before assisting their children. It made no sense to think that a mother would deprive her child of a breath for a second longer than she absolutely needed to. But if the mother passes out, the child is most certainly on his own. Without her own supply of oxygen, she can't take care of the one who depends on her for survival.

"I'm going to be taking a trip, Dad," I said.

"Oh, yeah? Where to?" he asked.

"Well, I've decided I'm going to ride my bike across the country."

"What?" he replied with a touch of skepticism in his voice. His glasses had slid a bit further toward the edge of his nose.

"Yeah. I had this idea when I was recovering from the ankle. Now that I'm better, I want to take advantage of the opportunity, and this summer feels like the perfect time."

My father was silent.

"I'm going to be taking three months off from work, a leave of absence," I added.

He remained quiet, blinking a couple of times, possibly still in disbelief.

"You can always call me," I said, reassuringly. "I want to make sure we stay in touch as much as possible. And I'm going to be lining up a bunch of people to visit you and check in on you."

Without taking a breath, my dad finally spoke. "Aren't you worried about tornadoes sweeping you off your bike in Kansas?" His eyes narrowed and the beginnings of a smile formed at the edges of his mouth. I exhaled with relief and grinned back at him.

Nine days later, on the morning of June 25, I began pedaling west from the steps of the US Capitol building. I had built a loose itinerary of roughly seventy-five days winding about four thousand miles to Seaside, Oregon, in a patchwork route that combined large sections of designated trails and roads recommended by the Adventure Cycling Association. I set up a blog entitled *Cambiophilia*, a term I made up roughly translated from the Latin for "love of change," and I pledged to take photos and write every day, uploading content from the iPad mini I toted as a luxury item. I had sublet my room in the third-floor apartment and nearly emptied my savings account to purchase a brand-new forest green Surly Long Haul Trucker. The sixty pounds' worth of gear I had loaded into front and rear paniers made the bike unfathomably heavy as I worked to turn the crank, but in that moment, I had never felt lighter.

Optimism carried me through that first day, even if my body wasn't up to the task. I had recognized the impossibility of training for the trek I was about to undertake, and instead, I simply suffered my way to fitness after starting my journey. For the first two weeks, each day brought some unique kind of ache or pain. Eight or more hours on the bike produced a tender wrist, a sore elbow, a stiff neck, or some form of unfortunate chafing. There were occasions when my ankle flared up, and there was even a day when I feared I might need to call off the trip for not having provided ample time to recover. Luckily, the ankle pain was short-lived, and eventually, my entire body settled in to a comfortable, familiar place atop the saddle like a baseball glove conforming to a hand.

A pleasant offset to my physical distress early in the journey, I was quickly exposed to the abundant generosity of strangers in incredible ways. On the second day of the ride, I rolled into Williamsport, Maryland, around one in the afternoon. I chose a quirky cafe with Wi-Fi called the Desert Rose for lunch and struck up a conversation with another cyclist sitting at the table next to me. John—or "Ski" as he was known—was headed from DC to Pittsburgh, and after a few minutes, we discovered our mutual connection to higher education. He was president of a large community college in Pennsylvania. After chatting for a while, we decided to ride together that afternoon as our planned accommodations for the night were about one block away from each other. We rode side by side the following day as well, talking about career, family, and biking. I shared with him a bit about my father and my reasons for riding across the country. After that discussion, I think Ski made a conscious decision to become the primary benefactor of my trip. That next night, he unexpectedly footed the bill for my hotel stay in Frostburg, Maryland. Even though we parted ways in the morning, we continued to stay in touch, and he followed my blog religiously. He asked for updates on my itinerary so he could find friends and colleagues in Podunk towns along my route that might be willing to feed me or house me for a night or two.

Though the days revealed fresh exciting stretches of road and trail that gave way to new places and new people, my mind held tightly to an apprehension about the future. I worried about getting lost, mechanical failure, and inclement weather. The worry was heavy—heavier than the bike itself—and it tainted my experience. It threatened to undermine the entire trip unless I learned how to manage it.

By the fifth day of the ride, I had reached West Virginia and found myself on a ten-mile stretch of what I believed to be the North Bend Rail Trail. What began as a paved bike trail transitioned into unpaved dirt, which then became single-track that deteriorated into muddy ruts. I lost confidence that I was headed the right way as the messy trail became no more than a narrow corridor of tall grass between thick forest on both sides. I pedaled through rough biking conditions until I reached a tunnel. Peering inside, I could see no daylight coming from the other end. I was incredibly doubtful as I looked into the darkness, but something was ushering me forward. I dug through my paniers to find my headlamp and clicked it to life as I rolled beneath the twenty-foot stone archway at the opening. I pedaled slowly but deliberately, my head jerking from the ground to the walls and up to the ceiling to visually assess the space that felt both cavernous and claustrophobic at once. The path below my tires changed from mud to rocks as I rolled over progressively larger stones. Puddles became wider and deeper, and before I realized it, I was pedaling through four inches of standing water. After a couple hundred yards of perfect blackness cut only by the beam of my headlamp, I saw the faint beginnings of daylight. I breathed a sigh of relief and pushed my way steadily through the rocks and water, the light of the other side beckoning me onward.

The tunnel was the kind of threshold I needed to finally immerse myself into the trip fully. Instead of fearing uncertainty, I began to lean into it. I started thinking about the future with more flexibility, mapping out no more than the next couple of nights' stays. I left more room for the unplanned and the unexpected. Getting lost might mean a few extra miles and a chance to see something strange. Not finding a restaurant for dinner would mean a gas station burrito or a protein bar from the depths of my paniers. I started to believe in my ability to figure it out if and when needed. That power had always been there, but I needed to have the faith in that power in order to tap it.

Later that day, I reflected on the tunnel and the many tunnels I had been through previously. They weren't always defined by darkness or distinct openings, but by uncertainty and isolation. A tunnel is a challenge in its most essential form. A tunnel is anything that requires a narrowing of focus to keep moving forward and a reliance on faith in oneself that reaching the other side is possible. The moments of obscurity and doubt in passage can be wildly oppressive and humbling, but they eventually lead to clarity and strength. My path as a caregiver for my father involved a series of tunnels, and sometimes it felt like one very long and very dark tunnel. It hadn't been until that day on my bike that I named it properly.

Frequent, selfless generosity from countless others would enrich the bike ride experience and affirm my belief in community. Ski was the first of many whose selfless actions made a world of difference in my trip. On the eighth day of the ride,

I reached Cincinnati, where a friend of a friend of a friend had offered to host me for a couple of nights. A physician and avid cyclist, John greeted me with open arms as I pedaled up his steep driveway to cap off a ninety-five-mile day. He told me to drop my bike off in the garage and then whisked me to his backyard patio, telling me a few of his friends would be stopping by to meet me. One by one, a dozen of his cycling buddies stopped by to hear tales from my first week on the trail as he and his wife delivered trays of delicious hors d'oeuvres for us to snack on. He set me up in their basement guest room and pulled an extra chair up to their dinner table that night, making me feel like I was part of their family.

The next day, John woke me up at 5 a.m., and we proceeded to go for an early fifteen-mile ride with a group called the Half-Day Café-ers, a crew of twenty or so middle-aged dads named after a tiny little coffee shop on Springfield Pike. Naturally, our ride ended there for an excellent cappuccino. Later on, John gave me the keys to his blue Prius so I could run a few errands and restock on supplies. That evening, he knocked on the door as I was packing up for my departure the next day. "Is that everything you have?" he asked, looking over my sorted piles of clothing.

"Yup, this is it," I replied.

"Wait here," he said, disappearing upstairs for a minute and then reappearing in the doorway. "Why don't you take these?" he asked, handing me one of the nicest cycling jerseys I had ever seen along with a pair of riding tights. "They don't fit me anymore, but I think they'll work for you."

Early the next day, July 4, it was raining buckets as I was preparing to leave. John opened the garage door to sheets of water splashing on the pavement outside. "Are you sure you don't want to stay one more day?" he asked.

Though the allure of sticking around for another day was strong, I felt an even stronger pull from the thousands of miles that still lay ahead. "Thank you for everything," I told him, pushing out of the garage and down his driveway, the familiar sound of my shoes clicking into the pedals mixing with the pitter-patter of raindrops.

***

A few days later, I pushed my way into central Missouri. I was just over a thousand miles deep into the trip and the days were starting to feel long and lonely. On July 10, I pedaled through misty conditions and arrived in Farmington, a small town on Adventure Cycling Association's Transamerica Trail. I ate lunch at a tiny eatery called Bauhaus Kaffee, opting for a club sandwich and a bowl of southwest chicken soup. As I was preparing to leave the little café, I saw a group of touring cyclists with loaded bikes gearing up to ride. They flagged me down and waved me to their side of the road. They, too, were headed west, and we set off together from that point.

The group of four, all in their mid- to late-twenties, included three guys living in Harrisonburg, Virginia, who had started their ride in DC a couple of weeks prior. They had met up with a fourth, a Brit with the hair and humor of Russell Brand, who had started his ride in Maine. We rode together, getting to know one another as we became familiar with the contours of the Ozark Mountains all afternoon and early evening, stopping only for shaved ice at a roadside stand on State Route 72. We rolled into the small village of Ellington at eight in the evening just as the only restaurant in town, a pizza place, was about to close. We ordered three pies loaded with toppings and grabbed a case of Busch

Light. We enjoyed our dinner alfresco on the curb outside the restaurant. As the sky turned a pale violet blue, we rode a mile down the road to a small public park where we set up camp under a picnic pavilion.

We rode and camped together for the next nine hundred miles, including some of the most unremarkable terrain I expected to encounter over the duration of the trip. That became comically apparent the day we stopped at a roadside pull-off in central Kansas with a sign that said, "scenic over-look." Beyond, there was nothing more than flat grassy fields stretching out to meet the horizon at a perfectly level line.

I was incredibly thankful for the companionship, as it brought a new kind of fullness and joy to the days. Being a part of a group also made us stronger and bolder. Before meeting up with the others, I had struggled to complete my first century day—a ride of one-hundred miles or more—and was skeptical of my ability to pull off the feat again. The two weeks of riding we did together included one day covering one hundred and twenty-four-miles, another covering one hundred and forty-four miles, and a third cranking two hundred miles through western Kansas and into eastern Colorado. Completing the double century on a fully loaded touring bike demanded more of me physically than I had ever known I had to give, but it also left me with the distinct belief that I was capable of so much more than I had previously thought.

I had deliberately chosen an east-to-west route to earn the benefits of the second half of the trip, and the natural landscape and topography of the American West proved a truly special reward. Pedaling toward Pueblo, Colorado, I remember seeing what I thought were a row of faint clouds reaching across a bluebird sky. Every few miles, however, clouds became more and more defined. When I realized I was looking at the outline of the white-capped ridge of the Front Range, I broke down and began to sob on my bike. I was looking at the Rockies.

I was overcome with emotion yet again as I made my way to Crested Butte, Colorado, where I was planning to take the better part of a week to relax and recharge with my brother and his girlfriend. This time, familiarity overwhelmed me with gratitude. Pedaling up Route 35 from Gunnison, I recognized the unmistakable A-frame of the house where Max and Garland rented a room. Shortly after, I spotted his lanky frame waving from atop his second-floor porch. I was far from Washington, DC, but I felt at home. After six days with Max and Garland hiking the local trails, eating home-cooked meals, and playing with their Jack Russel Terrier named Rusty, it was hard to get back on the bike and continue on my journey.

Just over a month later, I was rolling my bike past a statue of Meriwether Lewis and William Clark in Seaside, Oregon, on my way down to the beach to dip my front wheel in the Pacific Ocean. It had been seventy-three days since I left Washington, DC, and I had experienced something new each and every day. As a result, every day was instantly memorable; each day was its own unique adventure etched with vivid detail in my memory. Traveling by bicycle helped forge an intimate connection to the world around me—the road, the people, the plains and trees and mountains. Pushing myself physically and mentally each day—whether in distance, speed, or altitude gain—had cultivated a new and powerful mind-body connection.

There were countless new lessons for me to reflect on. When you commit to something big and bold, and you show that you have a plan and the discipline needed to execute it, people want to help you. I also realized I could wield my story to welcome that help. By the last third of the trip, if I hadn't yet settled on a place to stay that night, I'd head to the center of a town and lean my bike up against a gas station or grocery store. I'd break out my map, and then wait. Within minutes, I'd have at least one person ask me what I was up to, and from there, I could build a new and meaningful connection. It might mean sharing a drink or a meal, or finding a place to stay that night.

I learned that story is powerful, regardless of the context or the teller or the audience. If I didn't particularly like someone I met along the way, I'd withhold the best parts of the story about the trip. I'd keep secret the details that made the story unique and distinct. Some elements of the story of my bike ride were interesting but were clearly superficial. I rode a total of 4,267 miles, averaging about eighty miles per day of riding. I had ridden through fifteen states and crossed the Continental Divide eleven times. However, there was so much more in those miles.

I spotted a wolf drinking from a stream on the ascent to Willow Creek Pass outside of Walden, Colorado.

I was threatened by a man high on meth wielding a knife while setting up camp in a park in Pittsburg, Kansas.

I watched *The Goonies* for the first time during the night I spent in Astoria, Oregon, the town where the movie took place.

I turned down a ride from a stranger with a pickup truck, opting instead to take a calculated risk and race an approaching lightning storm in the vast, open plains of southwestern Wyoming.

I was passed by two beautiful naked women hiking the trail back from a hot springs that I was headed toward in the panhandle of Idaho.

I named my bike Justine in Green the Touring Queen, or simply Justine for short.

I took a "rest day" in Colorado Springs to run the Barr Trail to the summit of Pike's Peak in a borrowed pair of Asics sneakers.

I spent fifteen miles on I-80 in Wyoming in a windstorm, struggling to maintain control of the bike on a trash-covered median as tractor trailers buzzed by every half minute or so.

I reveled in the blissful taste of a can of room-temperature Del Monte diced pineapples that I discovered deep in the bowels of my paniers one blazingly hot afternoon when I had run out of water.

I made "gloves" out of socks and plastic bags to prevent my hands from going completely numb in thirty-four-degree rain while descending from the twelve-thousand-foot height of Independence Pass.

I came to recognize infinite depth in every story. There was more than could ever be shared. To tell one's story well is a nearly impossible task. For in the telling we are forced to create a shorthand, a shell that leaves out pieces for which words are inadequate, and that leaves out pieces we know might only resonate with ourselves because we lived it firsthand.

In September, I returned to DC stronger than I had ever been, possessing a completely new outlook on my life. I was about to start a new job that I had been excited about since receiving the offer via email while in rural Missouri. The day I got back home I took a few hours to visit my dad. The return to the Hebrew Home was instantly sobering. I had forgotten the stale smell of the hallways, the oppressive lighting, and the respectful aloofness of the receptionist at the front desk. It was sterile, artificial. The contrast to all of the places I had just been was aggressively stark.

Sitting on my father's bed beside his wheelchair, I pulled out of my backpack the iPad I had brought with me on my trip, the same iPad I had used to capture and share stories from the road. I opened the photo app and began leafing through images rhythmically, starting with the first day. I noted with surprise how different I looked in a photo atop Town Hill outside Flintstone, Maryland; I was clean shaven then, but began keeping a beard halfway through the trip. As I was sharing highlights from my passage through the tip of southern Illinois, I realized my father had been quiet since I started. I looked at him, but he refused to make eye contact with me. Suddenly, he was taking in heavy breaths, as if on the verge of tears. I knew he wouldn't admit it, but he was utterly sad, and though I'm sure there was some happiness for where I had gone and what I had done, the photos were horrific for him to look at. I dropped the iPad to my lap and clicked the sleep button to darken the screen.

"Let's finish looking at those later," I said. "How about we go outside for some fresh air?"

CHAPTER 11

"THEN GO!"

Returning from the cross-country bike ride was surreal. Having completed a life-altering and life-affirming adventure and preparing myself to return to nine-to-five employment, I felt a mix of contentment and discomfort, as if I had just finished a delicious meal at a restaurant where the air conditioning was a bit too cool on my skin. I wasn't excited to be back in DC, but I wasn't necessarily looking for more miles to ride either. I was in withdrawal, trying to find my place and my purpose as I floated around a post-travel purgatory. It was like that unsettling moment after getting home from the airport following a perfect vacation. Instead of unpacking, you just drop your suitcase in the middle of the floor and look at it, blank-faced.

Waiting for my flight to board back to Washington, I had done some research on the life of Meriwether Lewis. I was curious what the explorer did after returning from one of the most epic adventures in American history, especially after having followed the Lewis and Clark trail for a good portion of my ride through the western US. The year after returning from the expedition, Lewis was awarded 1,600 acres of land and was appointed governor of the Louisiana Territory by then President Thomas Jefferson. Two years later, Lewis was on his way to Washington, DC to deliver drafts of the Corps of Discovery journals, which he struggled to complete, and to recoup money he was owed by the War Department that had placed him severely into debt. He stopped at an inn outside of Nashville to rest one night, and before dawn the next morning, he was discovered on a buffalo skin rug having bled out from two gunshot wounds. Though there is some debate, it is largely accepted that Lewis died by suicide, historians placing his demise in the context of his heavy drinking, potential drug use, considerable debt, struggle to publish the expedition's journals, inability to find a partner for marriage, and the deterioration of his friendship with Thomas Jefferson.

Coming back to my third-floor apartment, I had found half a dozen packages stacked on my bed. Each wore the scars of extended journeys via standard shipping, emblazoned with their towns of origin. These were places where I jammed as much stuff as I could within a flat rate cardboard box and hastily taped it shut before sliding it across the counter: Harpers Ferry, Cincinnati, Colorado Springs, Crested Butte, and Portland. At each of those places, I reassured myself that I was better off with less, earning incremental confidence that I would be able to figure it out without the things that were more of a psychological crutch than of any practical use. With no more miles to ride and no more gear to jettison, I was left with just my memory of the ride and a void to fill in with the next project, the next adventure, and the next goal.

Two and a half weeks later, I was toeing the starting line at the 2014 Baltimore Marathon having signed myself up on a whim in the days following my return to DC. I had gotten a taste of endurance tests during the summer, and I reasoned that running was likely a more practical way to push myself than riding. Running would allow me to explore my limits during smaller blocks of time, much more feasible given the kind of schedule I kept. On top of that, I had caught the running bug listening to an audio version of Chris McDougall's *Born to Run* not once, but twice, as I twisted my way through the Rocky Mountains a few months back.

I didn't know exactly what to expect that day on the streets of Baltimore, but I did know that I was underprepared. I ran a few seasons of cross country in high school, but I acknowledged that this was a completely different beast. To train, I had gone on ten runs, the longest of which was fourteen miles. I did, however, know what it was like to challenge myself physically and mentally. I knew what it was like to ride a hundred, a hundred and fifty, and two hundred miles in a day, and what happened to my body and my mind as I became exhausted and the pain set in.

With the starting gun, I shuffled forward, packed in alongside a few thousand others, and eventually found a comfortable pace at around nine minutes per mile. I tried to ignore my watch and the distance markers, focusing instead on my form and my breathing. My mind became increasingly calm, and the tapping of my sneakers on the black asphalt placed me into a Zen-like trance. My senses heightened and my focus sharpened further as I got deeper into the course. I felt a boost of confidence passing the sign denoting fourteen miles, as each step marked the farthest I had ever gone on foot in a single run. Approaching the twenty-mile mark, the racers became more and more spread out, spectators dissipated, and a shroud of quiet hung in the air. Though I could see a few other runners in my field of vision, each of us was waging a private, personal war with distance and time. It was beautiful and moving and intensely motivating.

I crossed the finish line in three hours and fifty-five minutes, feeling exhausted but knowing I had it in me to keep going if I wanted.

I had been curious about distance running before the Baltimore Marathon, but I became fully committed in its aftermath. I wanted to do more miles, more races, and more boundary pushing. I wanted to return to the place I found deep in the marathon, and I wanted to go deeper.

The following Tuesday, I visited my father to share my experience of the race, and he smiled as I recounted the details. My father was an athlete right up until he was diagnosed with Parkinson's. He was a competitive amateur triathlete through his late forties, having tested his mettle in races like the Liberty to Liberty Triathlon. Held for years on July Fourth weekend in the mid-eighties, the event had entrants start with a ten-foot plunge off Liberty Island into the polluted Hudson River, swimming one and a half miles through rough chop and garbage, and then shuttled via ferry to the shores of Sandy Hook Bay. My father told me he had vomited as soon as he pulled himself out of the water, regaining his composure only a few minutes before embarking on the ninety-mile ride to downtown Philadelphia in eighty-five-degree heat. The race finished with a 10K run through the city to the Liberty Bell at Independence Hall.

When I was seven, my father signed me up for my first race, a one-mile fun run at South Mountain Reservation in West Orange, New Jersey. Among a few family photos in my collection, there's one from that day. I'm intensely focused on rounding a corner on the course, leaning forward aggressively in red shorts and Reebok Pumps while my father trails behind me, beaming with an ear-to-ear smile in a matching black tank top and running shorts.

"I used to have a trick when I was running," he told me in a scratchy voice, his eyes peering over the top of his black-framed glasses. His speech had notably declined over the summer, and I struggled to interpret some of his words.

"Oh yeah?"

"Yeah, and it always worked, too. When I was behind another runner in a race," he explained, "I would focus right between their shoulder blades, and I would try to absorb some of their energy."

I ate it up. My dad was giving me running tips. It was a wonderful new common ground for us to explore together. I told my father that I planned to sign up for more races, and that I was interested in trying my hand at a fifty-miler at some point that spring.

He seemed baffled by the concept, but he also wasn't discouraging. "Promise me you won't overdo it, though."

"Don't worry, Dad. I won't," I responded, his comments ripe with rationality.

"I want you to remember one thing, Josh," he told me sternly from his wheelchair. "You're a businessman first and an athlete second."

I found the statement odd, mostly because I was working at a nonprofit at the time. I understood the sentiment, but I wondered if he was really speaking to himself. Running offered me incredible value in its escapism. I was able to pull back from day-to-day reality and enter a focused state devoid of the cerebral buzz that clouded my mind. Running was also a way to distract from the continuous stream of worries that constantly threatened to overtake my days. I wondered if my father had used running as a tool in the same way I did, like a drug to relieve stress, to avoid responsibility, or to gain a relatively meaningless sense of accomplishment. Finishers medals didn't pay rent or fill the refrigerator.

***

The months that followed were a fast-paced blur of long days at the office, where I was settling into a new job that was both soul-serving and highly competitive given the talented and ambitious team I was working alongside. During evenings and weekends, I trained relentlessly, experimenting with workouts and nutrition to see how my body responded over time. I quickly came to the conclusion that if I wanted to run far, I needed to learn how to eat while running. Without calories, my body would begin to struggle, and I would hit lows sooner and for longer periods. One Saturday in early spring, I brought a burrito on a trail run and managed to consume it entirely before I completed the fifteen-mile loop through Rock Creek Park.

On April 12, 2014, I lined up with some three hundred other racers for the start of the Bull Run Run 50 Miler. It was a crisp spring morning, and I could feel the excited nervousness pulsing through the crowd. I hadn't gotten a great night's sleep the evening before, but I was as focused I could have been for that day. I placed myself toward the rear of the field for the start, and I resolved to stay as slow and steady as I could. My goal was to finish, and to do so on my own terms.

The aid stations were spread out every five to seven miles, and each one offered a moment to recharge. There was typically a spread of snacks that included peanut butter and jelly sandwiches, fresh fruit, chips, crackers, and various sports and soft drinks. I was running, but I also felt like the whole experience was a moving buffet. At the aid station at mile twenty-six, all of the race volunteers were dressed up in Christmas outfits, and they were peddling quesadillas, pierogis, and ramen noodles. It was everything I needed to push forward into the unknown. Save for one thirty-mile training run, I had never gone further than the marathon distance on foot.

At one thirty in the afternoon, I had reached mile thirty-three. I had been running for seven hours, but surprisingly, I felt fine. Looking at my watch and doing some quick math, I realized I had three hours to run seventeen trail miles if I wanted to finish in under ten hours. I thought about my goal of finishing on my own terms and decided to step on the gas a bit. I cut my pace down to ten minutes a mile and limited my time at aid stations to less than a minute. I started passing other runners who had slowed to a trot or who were pressing down on their knees as they made their way up the climbs.

I rolled into the last aid station of the course at mile forty-five. The warm weather and exhaustion were weighing me down, but I still had fifty-three minutes before the ten-hour mark. I still had a chance. As I filled up my water bottles, I racked my mind for an excuse to ease up and relax, but I couldn't find one.

An older, mustachioed runner who had taken a seat on a nearby picnic table must have sensed that confusion in my head and asked, "What's the problem, son?"

"Uh, there's no problem," I stammered, somewhat surprised by the question.

He looked at me wide-eyed and smiled. "Then go!" he said.

That quick exchange was all the boost I needed. I grabbed a fistful of ice to put under my hat and off I went.

Soon after, things started to get real. I had entered the part of the race I was looking for. I had found those excruciatingly revealing moments, and my personal internal battle. I had pushed my body to the edge of what I was capable of physically, and now it was time to will myself mentally through to the finish. After what seemed like an hour, I got to the base of a climb that I knew would take me up to Hemlock Overlook. This was the course's final "screw you" to the runners, a hundred-or-so-foot humbling ascent before the relief of the finish line. I looked up to the climb and then looked at my watch. Four minutes left.

I passed three dazed runners who were struggling to make it up the hill. By the time I made it to the top, my quads were searing. I weaved my way through the trees until I spotted the finish line a few hundred yards away down the gravel road. I gunned it, completely recharged with adrenaline, smiling as I ran down the chute to the finish line. I shook the race director's hand and breathed deeply. It was over. Hands on my knees, I glanced over at the clock, the bright red digits showing "10:00:55." I would have loved that first number to be a nine, but I was thrilled, nonetheless. And perhaps, I reckoned, this gave me a perfect reason to sign up for the next fifty-miler.

***

Around that time I started dating actively, taking advantage of several online platforms that helped to accelerate the process of meeting new people. In the six months that followed my bike trip, I went on first dates with at least three dozen women, producing the mix of outcomes and emotions that I think most young people in cities endure with online dating. Some consternation, some exasperation, some pleasure, and occasionally, some authentic enjoyment.

I was scrolling through my matches on OkCupid one Friday evening and came across a woman who had chosen the screen name "DeliberateLivin." I began drafting a message acknowledging the superiority of dark chocolate over its milk counterpart—which she noted in her profile—and my love of José Gonzalez's version of "Heartbeats," a song originally produced by The Knife—a band listed among her favorite music. A month later, after a few more messages back and forth, she finally gave me her phone number.

On July 11, 2014, I met Kate at A&D Bar on 9th Street in Shaw. We found a high-top table in the back and got to know each other over craft beer served in mason jars and French bread pizza. She had just completed graduate school at Tufts and was living in DC for the summer as she looked for her next job. She was perplexed but intrigued by my ultrarunning habit, though she eventually admitted that she had just bought a pair of running shoes somewhat begrudgingly. She asked me what I wanted to be when I grew up, and, feeling a sense of comfort, I told her I wanted to be a good dad. I told her a bit about my experience looking after my father, and somehow, she didn't get up and head for the door. Instead, she leaned into the conversation and wanted to hear more.

After almost three hours together, we walked outside to where our bikes were locked. I knew I desperately wanted to see Kate again, so I told her unabashedly. I moved in toward her and our lips met for a moment of bliss, and I pulled back to see her smiling widely.

"Have a good night," she told me, stepping her leg over her bike and pushing off down the sidewalk.

PART III

CHAPTER 12

ROUTINE MAINTENANCE

———

I was three hours deep into creating a PowerPoint presentation for a new project at the office when I realized the light entering my cubicle was hinting at a shade of amber. I glanced at the clock on the lower right corner of my computer screen. It was 5:45 p.m., and it was time to start wrapping up my work for the day.

After reaching an adequate stopping point twenty minutes later, I closed the lid of my laptop and zipped it within my backpack. I glanced around to see which of my colleagues were still present, but the office was empty save for a few individuals hunched over their desks at the far end of the floor. I turned and made my way to the elevator to start the trip out to see my father in Rockville.

A few blocks away, I descended the Farragut North escalator steps two at a time and transitioned into a jog toward the fare gate. Squinting at the station's LED sign above the platform, I could just barely make out the red and yellow letters, "6-car, Red, Shady Grove, 1 min." *Perfect timing*, I thought.

A minute later, I shuffled aboard alongside two suit-clad businessmen and reached for the handrail above my head. I swung my backpack around to the front of my body and unzipped the front pocket so I could retrieve my paperback copy of *The Road* by Cormac McCarthy. I opened to page seventy-seven to escape the confines of the subway car as we began accelerating away from the platform.

> *You wanted to know what the bad guys looked like. Now you know. It may happen again. My job is to take care of you. I was appointed to do that by God. I will kill anyone who touches you. Do you understand?*
> *Yes.*
> *He sat there cowled in the blanket. After a while he looked up. Are we still the good guys? he said.*
> *Yes. We're still the good guys.*
> *And we always will be.*
> *Yes. We always will be.*
> *Okay.*[3]

Some thirty-five pages and eleven stops later, the train had arrived at Twinbrook. We were above ground now, and the August sky showed off a brilliant gradient of pink and blue, with wispy clouds that reflected the electric orange of the sinking sun. As I stepped off the car, I thought of the father and son I was reading about in the book and wondered whether they were better off than my dad and me.

I found myself drawn to the post-apocalyptic genre because it was more fantasy than horror. In those stories, the characters' existence is boiled down to only the essentials: protect the ones you love, find enough food to survive, defend your home or keep moving, and avoid thieves, murderers, cannibals, and zombies.

---

3   Cormac McCarthy, *The Road* (New York: Alfred A. Knopf, 2006), 77.

As I hit the crossing signal request button on Rockville Pike, I wondered whether our reality was the real dystopia. I spent two-thirds of my waking hours between plastic and fabric partitions inside an office away from the people I love. My father was locked inside his Parkinsonian body and kept securely inside the confines of the nursing home, surrounded by unoffensive blue carpet, beige wallpaper, and too-bright fluorescent lighting. I had to travel fifty-minutes by transit and by foot to see him. Aside from my father's health condition, these realities were the result of choices I had made, but I was unaware of any real viable alternatives. I, nonetheless, clung to the notion that we could break free at any point. Beyond that, I'm not sure what we'd do to get by. I suddenly felt the familiar weight of practicality.

I pulled the door open to Panera Bread and stepped to the side as a mother and her son walked out into the warm evening air. The fast-casual eatery was full of diners: an elderly couple in khaki shorts and different colored polo shirts enjoying salads across from each other; a long-haired woman in her mid-twenties, alone, sitting with perfect posture typing intensely on her laptop; a father handing his toddler a plastic spoon so she could start digging into a cup of macaroni and cheese.

Occasionally, I would bring my father here, but tonight I'd be getting our meals to go. I never came to see my father empty-handed. I would always bring something, whether it was food, toiletries, clothing, magazines, or art supplies. The idea of bringing something was borne of a desire to get the most benefit out of each visit. My presence was delightful for my dad, I'm sure, but it didn't always make up for the fact that his days were horribly monotonous. He couldn't come and go as he pleased, and he ended his days falling asleep on a rubber mattress.

"Order number ninety-three," announced a young man from behind the counter who couldn't have been more than eighteen. His name tag was adorned with smiley face stickers surrounding the name, "Dor."

"Thanks," I said, picking up the brown bag from atop the counter.

I looked inside to check the order: two half turkey sandwiches, a cup of black bean soup, a cup of cream of chicken and wild rice, two bags of kettle chips, and two chocolate chip cookies. It was all there, just as it was every week I went through this routine.

I crossed the parking lot of the Federal Plaza strip mall to the cutout in the fence at the edge of the Miramont Apartment complex. The sky was glowing light indigo above me while I walked through the field adjacent to the Bender JCC of Greater Washington. Gazing to my right, I saw t-ball practice was underway as a bunch of four and five-year-olds were being corralled and repositioned by hovering parents.

I reached the front desk of the Hebrew Home and lifted the pen to sign in. The clock behind the receptionist showed 7:14 p.m. Turning around, I could see that the lobby was void of any residents or visitors. It was expectedly quiet this evening, as it was most every evening.

Entering room 520, I found my dad asleep in his wheelchair, slumped forward and to the side, forehead suspended an inch above his left armrest.

I crouched next to him and put a hand gently on his shoulder. "Hey, Dad. How are you?"

He slowly began to straighten up and blinked a few times, setting his eyes on mine. "Josh, you're here." He pulled his arms up to the armrests and pressed himself up further. When sitting "up," his head still appeared to be coming forward at a right angle from between his shoulders.

"How was dinner?" I asked.

"Bubbe's baked chicken, again," he said unenthusiastically.

"Ah, Bubbe strikes again! I'm sorry to hear that." I had tried a piece off his plate once. It was noticeably overdone, and I had the urge to sprinkle salt over the rest of my dad's dish. Unfortunately, the nursing home didn't put saltshakers out on the tables in an effort to maintain strict nutritional standards for residents. "Lucky for you, I've got contraband."

"Great. Can you do my nails before we eat?"

"Sure thing," I said, reaching in my backpack and pulling out the nail clippers I kept there at all times for just such a purpose. I repositioned his chair adjacent to the bed and had a seat atop the mattress. I pulled the rolling table in front of him and placed his left hand atop the light wood veneer.

Trimming my father's nails was one of the important rituals we carried out on a regular basis. The nursing staff did so much more for my father than I could ever express my appreciation for; and while I considered tending to my father's nails as an intimate act of service to him, it was also a small token of gratitude for the staff who took care of him during the vast, vast majority of time I wasn't present.

"How's your flexibility?" I asked.

"Not great," my father responded. He flexed his fingers out slowly to their maximum extent; however, they were still curved as if wrapped around an invisible baseball.

I gradually pushed his palm down on the table using the heel of my hand, stretching his fingers carefully. My father's skin was yellowish and speckled, covered with freckles and the marks of age. His knuckles were pronounced, calloused and constantly swollen from impact. Since he couldn't get his fingers out in time, he would use a fist to dampen his falls.

One by one, starting with this thumb, I worked deliberately to cut back the thick and gunk-filled nails, attempting to keep tabs on the clippings before they jumped too far. By the pinky, my father was asleep and lightly snoring, with his head tilted back and his mouth wide open. I could see the dark fillings in his bottom molars.

I carefully lifted up my dad's right hand. It was in much worse shape than the left one, mostly numb and perpetually folded in on itself. The root causes of this condition are hard to pinpoint, but I linked them to an initial incident more than fifteen years prior during which my father fell and dislocated his shoulder while getting off the subway in New York City. While sitting in an emergency room waiting hours to be seen, he gradually lost feeling in his hand, and it never fully returned.

The rigidity brought on by the Parkinson's, coupled with years of atrophy from disuse, rendered his hand almost entirely unusable. I had attempted to goad my father into wearing a brace to keep the hand open while he slept, but it proved too difficult and too painful for him to manage.

I turned the hand over and gently pried his fingertips away from his palm. As I opened up the hand, I discovered that the crease of the palm opposite from the thumb was white with what looked like athlete's foot. I made a mental note to tell the charge nurse on my way out that she needed to address that. I began trimming the nail of his right thumb while my father was still asleep. The ring finger was a bit tricky—that nail had grown in with a split since an accident with a sawblade decades ago.

With the hands complete, I pushed the table away and bent over toward my father's feet. As I got closer, the smell nearly froze me in place. I had forgotten to brace myself for the stench, invariably made worse by the lack of socks on my dad's feet. Shoes without socks was becoming more and more common for him. My father would stubbornly resist help in getting dressed, and after the essentials like underwear, pants, and a shirt were covered, he'd insist on doing the socks himself. However, they were arguably the hardest. If they made it on in the morning, it was a success. But if, for any reason, they came off during the day, they would stay off.

I removed the right shoe and propped my father's right leg up on my knee. The foot was exceptionally arched and the toes were pulled inward, ostensibly the result of chronic cramping brought on by the Parkinson's and, like his hands, the result of atrophy from immobility. Purple and blue veins were visible through his skin, and the nail on his big toe was the same shade as a pale egg yolk. I worked steadily through each toe and repeated the effort on his other foot. My father woke up as I was getting his sneakers back on.

I checked my watch to see that it was seven thirty. I got up to wash my hands in his tiny in-room half bathroom. "How about some food, Dad?" I asked. After years of assisting my father with his hygienic practices, the prospect of eating shortly after handling his feet didn't faze me as much as it potentially should have.

"Sounds good," he responded, shifting in his wheelchair.

Returning to his side, I pulled the rolling table back into place and started emptying the contents of the brown bag from Panera. I opened the wax paper enclosing the sandwich and dumped the chips out of their bag, making sure everything was accessible. I opened my father's black bean soup and set it down in front of his left hand so he'd be able to lift it to his mouth and drink it from the cup when ready.

I grabbed the remote control and pulled up the channel guide. I hit the arrow repeatedly until TBS was highlighted and hit "Select." *Seinfeld* had just started. Though it had been in syndication for over a decade and we had individually probably seen every single episode, we both still laughed like it was the first time.

They were showing the episode where Jerry and Elaine visit Mr. and Mrs. Seinfeld in Florida. Jerry's dad, Morty, was the guest of honor at the annual dinner for the outgoing condo association president, and Jerry was asked to provide entertainment. Rather than being a happy occasion, a series of unfortunate events led up to a dinner that went horribly wrong. At the climax of the show, Morty's frustration boiled over and he assaulted the event emcee and rival alpha male, Jack Klompers.

At that moment, my father belted out a hearty carefree laugh and looked over at me without worry. It was one of those rare moments when I could tell he was genuinely happy. And that made me happy. *Seinfeld* had that kind of effect on my father and me, and for good reason.

When I was a kid, my parents and I used to watch the show as it aired live on Thursday nights. I sat between them on their bed, eagerly awaiting the next punchline. It was bliss. To have my mother on my left, my father on my right, and the *Seinfeld* crew in front of me was the best combination of comfort and entertainment that I could imagine. There was warmth, simplicity, and ease in that memory.

I also distinctly remember the opening sequence to *L.A. Law*, the legal drama that came on right after *Seinfeld*. To this day, the theme song still reminds me of one thing—the disappointment of bedtime.

My father would follow me into my room across the hall. I would climb into bed and demand to be tucked in. Occasionally, I would ask him to tuck me in on all sides, mummy style. I would tell him to leave the door cracked open just a few inches, allowing the glow of my parents' television to spill over my blanket and tint the fur of the stuffed animals that kept me company. I couldn't quite hear the TV from that far away, but I would watch the characters move across the screen until my eyelids were too heavy to keep open.

The scene had changed dramatically since then. The unique and familiar warmth of my parents' bedroom had been replaced by the impersonal, sterile setting of my father's room at the nursing home. My father's bed was much smaller and much less comfortable now. Most importantly, when it was time for bed, I was tucking my father in and not the other way around.

At the very end of the episode, Elaine's back went out and a chiropractor told her she needed to stay an additional three days at Jerry's parents' place to recover. My father let out another throaty laugh as the credits began to roll.

I spent the next fifteen minutes chatting with my father and tidying up his room: folding clothes and setting them inside his chest of drawers, putting away his toiletries, and picking up shirts that had slid off the hangers in his closet. I turned to my father, who had finished all of his food and was now looking drowsy again. I took it as my cue to start my departure.

"Alright, Dad," I said, grabbing a pair of blue cotton pajama pants and a fresh t-shirt from his dresser. "I think I'm gonna head out. Let me help you get into bed."

I applied the brakes to the wheelchair and pulled the sneakers off his feet once again. I positioned myself in front of his knees and leaned over, putting my hands in his armpits. I gave him a count, "One, two, three," and then lifted his torso up and toward me.

I helped him stay upright while shifting his backside to the edge of his bed and then lowered him slowly to the mattress. I reached around his waist and lifted him up just enough to pull his heather gray sweatpants down to his ankles and off his feet. I noticed a few wet spots where the black bean soup had been spilled as I tossed the pants into the hamper. I positioned the pajama pants around his ankles and pulled them up to his waist.

"Lift up your arms," I instructed. He raised his elbows a few inches as I peeled the t-shirt up and over his head. My father's shoulders were broad, and there were deep pockets in the skin next to his collarbones. The battery for my father's neurostimulator—a perfectly square box raised half an inch from the skin around it—protruded wildly from his chest. The lead wire made its way from the device upward, disappearing beneath the flesh as it reached his neck.

In his continuous slouch, my father's back was curved and compressed, drastically shortening the height of his abdomen. I unfurled the shirt and pulled my father's limbs through the openings one arm at a time and then settled it over his head. I pulled his legs up and helped him swivel so his back was toward the head of the bed before lowering him gently to his pillow.

I went to the foot of the bed and adjusted the setting so he was propped up at a near forty-five-degree angle. I pulled my father's sheet and thin woven blanket up over his legs and to his chest. I grabbed the remote control to the TV and left it at his side.

"See you in a few days," I said, grabbing my backpack from the floor beside his wheelchair.

"Take care, Josh."

I ran my hand over his sparse hair and kissed his scarred and spotted forehead. "Good night."

Outside the Hebrew Home, the sky was a dark violet. I made my way back to the Twinbrook Station, where the sign indicated a thirteen-minute wait for the next red line train to Glenmont. I glanced down the length of the platform. A couple of teenagers were huddled closely together, listening to music playing from one of their cell phones. I found a seat on a concrete bench close by and cracked the pages of *The Road* where I had left off.

CHAPTER 13

ONE HUNDRED PERCENT

———

I reviewed the items neatly arranged on my floor: a bright blue foam roller, three pairs of sneakers with progressively thicker soles, a lightweight mesh running vest surrounded by multiple water bottles of various shapes and sizes, a headlamp, eight pairs of socks, anti-chafing cream, a bottle of electrolyte pills, a blister repair kit, and a small bottle of Advil Liqui-Gels. Checking them off my packing list, I started tossing each of the items into a large duffel bag. Turning to my dresser, I pulled a few moisture-wicking tops out of the drawer along with a couple of pairs of running shorts. *I think I'll go with the blue ones on race day,* I thought.

Atop my dresser was the coup de grâce: a custom trucker with "J-O-S-H" screen printed in big bold black letters that had just arrived a few days prior. I figured if I was going to be running a hundred miles in a state I had never been to, it couldn't hurt to give folks watching a name they could use when cheering. I had a feeling, too, that I would need as much support as possible to reach the finish line.

As I zipped the duffle, I thought back to the moments in the prior weeks when I had attempted to explain why I had signed up for the Rocky Raccoon One Hundred-Mile

Endurance Run. For nearly everyone who asked, my explanations were woefully insufficient. The conversations were usually brief, and I was typically labeled crazy in short order. I thought, maybe, that the "crazy" label was a bit of a defense mechanism proffered by those who were made uncomfortable by the mention of running one hundred miles. On the eve of the race, however, I had reached a conclusion that gave me all the comfort and confidence I needed. It didn't matter what other people thought. Affirmation was unnecessary, and arguably, irrelevant.

Regardless of judgment from others, my reasons were crystal clear. I was doing it because I had completed ultras at the fifty-kilometer and fifty-mile distance, and I believed I was ready for one hundred miles. I had wanted something truly difficult to work for, and I had worked very hard to prepare for it. I wanted to venture even deeper into the abyss that I had discovered late in the ultramarathons I had run, and experience, yet again, the transformation and self-reveal that was otherwise impossible to find. I was scared of what might happen, but overcoming that fear presented a peculiar allure. I had watched my father fall apart, and I wasn't going to take for granted my ability to run far distances while I had it.

The next day, I was lugging my bag through the Houston International Airport, butterflies already active in my stomach despite the fact that there were still thirty-six hours before the start. On the shuttle to the rental car center, I noticed a woman with sneakers tied to a large, teal duffle bag.

"You aren't running Rocky Raccoon, are you?" I asked.

"I am indeed," she told me. "I'm Emily."

Emily was a seasoned ultra-runner with multiple fifty and one-hundred-mile finishes under her belt. We hadn't seen each other on the plane, but we had both come from Washington, DC on the same flight.

"I don't like taking advice from anyone, but I'll share some anyway since this is your first hundred," she said. "Eat as much as you can between now and the race, and make sure you go slow. Slower than you ever thought you needed to go."

The next morning, I worked a bit from my room at the Days Inn and then headed to Huntsville State Park to go for a short shake-out run. Those couple of miles allowed me to see a bit of the trail, breathe the air, and feel the surface I'd be running on for at least part of the course. Later, I picked up my friend Kyle from the airport. He had flown in from New Haven to crew me for the weekend.

Crewing is easily one of the most thankless jobs in existence. During the race, if all went to plan, I would only see Kyle five times for a few minutes apiece. His job was to run through a full checklist to make sure I was addressing hot spots and blisters on my feet, that I wasn't ignoring chafing and soreness, and that I was getting enough calories, salt, and water. He was tasked with offering reminders to prevent me from making stupid mistakes, and most importantly, to prevent me from moving too fast.

The next day, we woke up at four in the morning, two hours ahead of the starting gun, and headed over to IHOP. I pounded French toast and bacon, though I felt like I hadn't even begun to digest the stuffed chicken marsala, mashed potatoes, and chocolate cake I gorged on less than eight hours before at Olive Garden.

The race start was surreal. I had calmed myself down to the point where I had almost forgotten the gratuitousness of the task before me. In my naive inexperience, I completely neglected to consider the fact that it would still be dark at six in the morning. I needed to borrow Kyle's headlamp since the one I brought for myself had been stowed in the drop bag I sent to an aid station called Damnation several miles away. Without Kyle's light, I would have been in serious trouble. After a quick hug, I made my way to the mass of runners crowded behind the starting line.

The Rocky Raccoon course was set up as five laps of twenty miles each. Aid stations were peppered in about three to six miles apart, and runners saw four aid stations before coming back to the start/finish turnaround at Dogwood. I would never be too far from food, water, or volunteer support. I figured that was great because I didn't need to carry more than thirty ounces of water with me at any given time. Mentally, however, a course like this can be tricky to navigate. It can become monotonous, tiresome, and easy to quit after each twenty-mile interval.

At the gun, all four hundred runners began shuffling forward in the dark. The first three miles were a crawl. Despite the pace, I still managed to stumble a few times on roots and rocks. It took me almost an hour to reach the first aid station, and I worried I had stuck myself between runners who were moving too slow. I felt an urge to move up in position but quickly reminded myself that I still had ninety-seven miles to go and almost laughed out loud.

I ran for a bit alongside a guy who was running Rocky Raccoon for the fifth time, having failed to finish during each of his first four attempts. I was shocked that someone would be so stubborn as to try something for the fifth time after failing four times; but in reality, anyone even thinking of running a hundred miles has to be stubborn as hell.

The first loop, as many described it would be, was fairly effortless. It was an introduction to the course, and despite the fact that the first few miles were slow due to the log-jam of runners who crowded the single-track trail, it still went by fairly quickly. I came back into the turnaround at Dogwood, dumped my headlamp, refilled my water bottles, and restocked my supply of Honey Stinger Waffles. After a five-minute check-in with Kyle, I was back out for loop two.

Shortly after, about twenty-two miles into the race, I began to feel some minor aches and pains. The lateral ligaments in my knees were a bit sore, and a spot on my right forefoot was causing me some discomfort. I remember saying to myself that they were just wrinkles I was ironing out, and eventually, that pain gradually went away.

I bumped into Emily at the Damnation aid station at mile twenty-six. Recognizing her experience and the ever-so-slight beginnings of doubt creeping into my head, I decided to run with her through the remainder of the loop. She was a calming, leveling presence and coached me to walk even the most gradual of uphill sections to preserve my legs. We worked slowly and steadily to cover the miles. The loop was slower than I wanted, but I was fine with that. I was feeling okay coming back into the turnaround at Dogwood, and that was the most important thing. I re-upped on water, food, and salt, before changing my socks. Feeling a few hot spots, I decided to ditch my thin merino socks for some thicker cotton ones. I felt like I had brand new skin on my feet.

The third loop began on a low note. While my feet were refreshed, I was starting to feel my first real down period. I was physically feeling fatigued and my mind was starting to grapple with the notion that I had been running for nine hours and I wasn't yet halfway done. I tried to break down the remaining sixty miles into a series of checkpoints. I focused on the twenty-mile loop I was running, about the distance to the next aid station, about the steps to next turn in the trail, about the tree fifty feet ahead. Whatever it took to refocus on the most imminent measurable milestone I could realistically envision.

Within a few miles, I was feeling better. I was still with Emily, and we were steadily making our way. We'd walk the uphills, jog the flats, and run the downhills. We talked about training and racing, but also veered toward topics like work, dating, family, and more. For two people who didn't know each other before, the conversation became incredibly candid and honest as we pushed ourselves past the fifty-mile mark. It was part confession, part interview, part reflection, and part commiseration. We shared our suffering as we shared ourselves.

Around mile fifty-three, Emily stepped off the trail to go to the bathroom, telling me to press on ahead. Though she said she'd catch up to me, I decided I would up the pace a tad. The sun had dipped below the horizon, and the sky was fading to a light violet. Just as I was beginning to get excited about the prospect of going slightly faster, I reached my second low of the race, and it lingered with me for the last five miles of the loop right until I rolled into Dogwood. The only saving grace in that moment was the thought of reconnecting with Kyle and having him jog with me for the first few miles of the next loop.

I kept the same socks and shoes for loop four because I knew that if I took them off, I wouldn't like what I was going to see. My feet were beginning to develop some serious blisters, mostly between the toes. At this point, I wasn't going to pop them. My plan was to keep them intact and push past any pain.

After restocking my supply of food and water, Kyle joined me as we left Dogwood. He ran the windy 3.1 miles to the Nature Center aid station and then took a direct route back to the turnaround. We were making okay time—roughly twelve minutes per mile—which was in line with my plan to push myself a bit for the loop. My philosophy was that it didn't matter if I went too fast on this loop because I would be fueled by adrenaline and the desire to finish on the final loop. At that point, I was also very conscious of the possibility that I could finish in under twenty-four hours. We left Dogwood at 7:55 p.m., which gave me ten hours for the last two loops. I remember thinking that if I could get back there by twelve thirty in the morning, I would have five and a half hours for the last loop, which would be plenty of time.

As I continued on, I kept thinking about how jealous I was of people on their last loop. I wanted to be done, but I still had more than twenty miles to go. At that point, the pain in my legs had set in for good. There were no particular sources of soreness because everything was sore. However, I knew how to combat the pain. Physiologically, I needed to stick to my intake plans to ensure I didn't cause any avoidable mistakes. I had to stay on top of food, salt, and hydration like a hawk. Mentally, I needed to get over the negative sensation, to put the pain in the background. It was there, but I needed to focus instead on willing myself to move forward. The pain didn't matter as much as getting closer to the finish.

I rolled back into Dogwood around a quarter after twelve with plenty of time left to finish before the twenty-four-hour mark at six in the morning. I had deliberately avoided sugar, caffeine, and energy gels until this point, but it was time to start taking the high-octane stuff. I loaded my vest with a handful of gels, took an Advil, and got back on the trail. Kyle joined me for the first three miles of the loop once again. Just before one in the morning we hit the Nature Center aid station. I gave him a high five and told him I would see him soon.

After parting ways with Kyle, I was left to stare down the final seventeen miles of the race on my own. The distance to the finish was a brutal, raw void. I had heard other ultrarunners talk about how the sport strips you down to your soul, but I didn't understand what that meant until I was there at that moment. My emotions during the race were an iceberg. At the start, I could see the contours of the ice above the water, but eighty miles on foot brought into view what was hidden beneath the surface. The visible had seemed so significant at first, but the immensity of the hidden emotional journey I discovered deeper into the race changed my perception drastically. As I came to acknowledge that I had begun to race more with my mind than my legs, the world around me fell under the dark shroud of nighttime.

The longest I had run in a given stretch prior to Rocky Raccoon was fifty miles, but those races were over within the span of a day and run entirely in daylight. The hundred-mile distance meant I would be in the dark for hours. I had started before dawn, watched the sun rise, run all day, watched the sun set, then run another fifty miles in the dark. Running by headlamp light was both deeply isolating and frustrating. I had very little context of where I was going other than my memory of the trail from earlier in the day. I had ridden my bike across the country largely on my own, and I don't think I ever felt as lonely as I did during stretches of the race during the night.

During the Damnation loop (miles eighty-six to ninety-two), I had my last major low of the race. I made a conscious decision to slow my pace and stay twenty feet behind a man and woman who were running and chatting with one another. Like a creep, I ran behind them for more than an hour but didn't say a word to them. I stayed with them because I needed to be around other people. My instincts told me to hitch my wagon to theirs for a bit because I felt like I couldn't handle being alone, and following people was ever-so-slightly easier than following a trail. It allowed my brain, my most valuable muscle at that point, to rest a bit before I knew I would need it again to close out the race.

The miles that followed were full of fear and doubt. The darkness filled me with loneliness, despite my proximity to the two runners just a few body lengths ahead. My mind wandered to my father. It was both painful and inspiring to dwell on his existence. I thought about his room at the Hebrew Home, those four walls forming the extent of his universe. I thought about his window view of the parking lot, and the trees just beyond. I reminded myself of gifts I was celebrating by running through the woods of Huntsville State Park at three o'clock in the morning, of the lessons I would learn from this experience and of my ability not just to recover, but to become stronger, from this suffering.

Back at Damnation (mile ninety-two), I reconnected with another racer I had met earlier who was also running his first hundred-miler. We had run together for a bit, and I had gone ahead of him, but now he had caught up. He left me at the aid station telling me he was going for a sub-twenty-three-hour finish. He wasn't going very fast, but I watched him leave thinking there was no way I could stick with him.

At that point in the race, walking meant allowing my body to stiffen up. It hurt to run, but considering the fact that I would continue to get stiffer and stiffer if I walked, it was worth it to run at a pace marginally faster than a walk.

To my surprise, however, after a few hundred feet, marginally faster led to considerably faster; and rather than stopping to walk the uphills as I had previously done, I committed to running everything.

I got to Park Road aid station, and as I had done on each loop previously after leaving the station, I made a quick check-in call to Kyle to let him know I was on the home stretch. It was 4:02 a.m., and my dear friend was still awake, still waiting for me to finish this obscenely long race. After hanging up, a switch flipped in my mind. Perhaps it was the music I had pumping through my headphones, the coffee-flavored energy gel I slurped down, or the soda I chugged at Park Road. Perhaps it was the desire to get out of the dark, hug my friend, take a shower, and go to sleep as soon as possible. Perhaps it was the adrenaline that coursed through my veins as I began to visualize the finish.

I started running as if I hadn't just run ninety-five miles. I started running as if I was fresh. I was a machine, and I was flying over the dirt and between the trees. I was sweating and breathing harder than I had the entire race. I felt a primal urge to hunt down the runners in front of me, to pass them with abandonment. I had never been freer in my life. I felt good enough to get myself to the finish line at that pace, and if I didn't, I would slow down. But I never slowed down. I ran the uphills, I charged through the flats, and I blazed the downhills. I was passing people every twenty seconds or so, some nearing the finish themselves and others on earlier laps. Many had brief words of encouragement as I pressed forward: "Looking good!" "Great work!" "Go get 'em!" One woman just said, "Wow."

I rounded the corner to the last hundred-yard chute into Dogwood and the finish, sprinting with everything I had.

I crossed the timing pad for the fifth and final time as the chip strapped around my ankle triggered a subtle beep. One hundred miles in twenty-two hours thirty-four minutes and twenty-nine seconds. I was simultaneously elated, grateful, and depleted beyond imagination. My mind felt like it had spent a full day shaken up in a washing machine while my body had been tumbling in the dryer.

Kyle drove our rental car back to the Days Inn while I melted into the passenger seat and attempted to parse out the race. My primary goal was to finish on my own terms. My secondary goal was to finish in under twenty-four hours. I had considered it a privilege to even toe the starting line at Rocky Raccoon, and I was thankful for such a beautiful, brutal, and revealing experience. The race had proven that successfully running an ultra is about knowing myself: when to eat, when to drink, when to walk, when to run. Not just how to feel pain, but to understand it. Not just how suffer, but how to process it and how to respond. It had also proven that I was capable of so much more than I had previously assumed. That there was so much more untapped potential within me. Unless I made the decision to tap it, I would never see it. I wasn't sure if I would ever run another hundred-miler, but I knew I wanted to take a long time to reflect on that first one. I recognized I can only do something for the first time once, and I'm glad I made this first time count for so much.

Unloading my gear back at the hotel room with Kyle, I noticed a voicemail on my phone from an unknown number. Pushing play, I instantly recognized Kate's voice. She was mid-way through an assignment abroad in rural South Sudan, and she had called from her satellite phone.

"Hello, Josh. You're probably running right now, and I hope you are enjoying every step," she said. "I just wanted to let you know I was thinking about you, and I was proud of you."

I smiled listening to the recording. Kate was one of those few people who had immediately understood why I was running this race.

"I have a feeling you are going to do great. I can't wait to hear about it."

CHAPTER 14

WATCH AND LEARN

———

My mother once told me, "With enough time, you can get used to anything." Her words were simultaneously a testament to the resilience of human beings as well as a horrible reminder of just how little control we have over our lives, and that often, we simply have to put up with things. As my father lost more and more control over his body, I got the sense that most of his existence was about putting up with things, and occasionally, to lean on help when things became unbearable on his own.

Over time, as a result of his decline, my dad become more and more of an observer of the world and less of a participant. His ability to interact with everyone and everything around him was diminishing, as if an athlete being pulled back from the field of play, first to the sidelines, then to the stands, and then to the parking lot outside the stadium. It was difficult to witness, and it was even more difficult seeing the fight in my father progressively diminish as he was giving in.

But still, even from his wheelchair, my father retained his ability to observe and evaluate, if not to react and engage. After a family friend donated a desktop computer to my dad, I sensed he was grateful to have a piece of technology in his room other than the television. The physical presence of the computer, and the idea of the computer as a portal to the outside, was more valuable than the actual machine itself. Given the extremely limited dexterity in his hands, I didn't get the sense that my father had been using it at all in the recent months.

The television offered the kind of soothing one-way engagement that so many of us find comforting, even anesthetizing. When I came to visit my dad, I often found him watching. When our conversations got stale, we found a good show or a game to watch. When our visits were done, I always left the television on for him. That television was always there for him. And perhaps that provided some secondary benefit in the form of reassurance to me. It was part of the reason I happily paid far too much money for his cable bill each month.

The computer and the television, along with the entirety of the world around my father, were squarely dependent on his vision. My father had required corrective lenses his entire adult life, wearing contacts up until he was diagnosed with Parkinson's. At that point, he switched exclusively to glasses since they didn't require the precise routine of getting lenses in and out of his eyes. Though glasses may have been easier than contacts, they still presented challenges. Despite my best efforts, he always seemed to lose or destroy every single set of frames he owned. He would sit on them, roll over on them after falling asleep with them on, or drop them on the floor and crush them with his wheelchair. Dozens of pairs of glasses had been damaged beyond repair over the years. Though his prescription had leveled out, and I had gotten into the familiar routine of buying him a new set of glasses every couple of months, he was still occasionally letting me know that he couldn't see properly.

By February of 2016, my father was regularly complaining about his eyesight. "You need to take me to the eye doctor," he told me during a visit. "I'm seeing dark spots, and everything is fuzzy."

"Well, we might need to get your prescription adjusted," I said, wheeling him into the harsh white light of his tiny blue-tiled bathroom. "Your left eye looks like it might be a little cloudy. We should get that checked out."

I knew it couldn't be good as I rolled him back over to the adjustable table in the middle of the room. His peripheral awareness was severely impaired, and that was becoming painfully clear. I dumped a bag of potato chips in front of him, and he blindly reached for them, instead grabbing the bag they came in, bringing it to his mouth, and attempting to chew. It was strange and sad, to say the least.

I arranged for an eye exam at the Visionworks a short drive from the Hebrew Home. The following week, I borrowed my roommate's canary yellow 1990 Jeep Cherokee and drove out to Rockville to pick Dad up. Foolishly, I gave myself only twenty minutes to retrieve him and get him over to the appointment. I chronically underbudgeted transition time when taking my father to appointments, adding unnecessary stress to an already stressful situation.

After reaching the fifth floor, I found my father watching TV in the main sitting room beside a row of other residents in their wheelchairs.

"I think I need a change," my father said before I could open my mouth to greet him.

I wheeled him to his room, got new clothes out of his drawer, took off his shoes, stood him up, held him balanced in place, dropped his pants, sat him down, took the pants off his legs, stood him back up, took his diaper off, sat him back down, threw the diaper in the trash, gave him a quick wipe down, put new underwear around his legs, stood him back up, slid the underwear up to his hips, sat him back down, put new pants around his legs, stood him back up, pulled the pants up, and buttoned the waist. I grabbed an old, stained Carhartt jacket from the closet, got it on one arm, looped it around his back, and slid his other arm in. We were all set.

I wheeled my dad out to the parking lot and rolled him up to the passenger door of the Jeep. As if a heavily choreographed dance, I maneuvered dad into the front seat, folded up his wheelchair, and threw it into the trunk. We drove the five minutes to Visionworks and parked just outside. I unloaded the wheelchair, got my father situated, and made our way for the door.

As we rolled in, I realized I may have made a tactical error by moving too quickly. I didn't find out when my father's next dose of medication was due, and it's possible I left without requesting the pills he needed from the nurse on his unit. Without his Sinemet, which my father took every few hours, he would become essentially immobile and painfully uncomfortable. I kept my fingers crossed that this would be relatively quick, and we'd have him back in less than an hour.

After checking in, we waited about ten minutes before being called back to pre-exam. Everyone who has had an eye exam knows the tests they put you through. You lean into that large machine and trace images on the screen to gauge your eyesight or your astigmatism. They warn you about the puff of air they blow into your eye before searching it, and you sit there quietly taking it like a champ. These tests were nearly impossible for my dad because he couldn't sit up straight. For him to effectively lean forward and put his chin onto the chin rest and get his forehead against the forehead rest, I needed to lean against him with all my weight while keeping his head straight. And still, with me propping him up and holding him perfectly still, Dad wasn't able to keep his eyes open long enough to do the tests properly. The tech working with my dad was incredibly patient—more patient than I could have hoped for. Still, it was a struggle creatively positioning my father to meet the needs of the moment while accepting the very real limitations of this process to accommodate for someone in my dad's condition. It took about twenty-five minutes to complete the red balloon test and to take less-than-perfect images of his retinas. As a result, we didn't even attempt to get the puffs of air into his eyes.

Defeated, I wheeled my father back into the waiting area. It was typically hard to read my father's feelings, but I could tell he was frustrated. "Are you okay?" I asked. He didn't respond. He just stared a few feet ahead of himself on the ground. So far, our visit had been challenging at best, and at worst, it was yet another reminder of his body failing him.

When we made it into the exam room, the doctor, a light-haired woman in her late forties with red-framed glasses, had pushed the chair out of the way so dad could remain in his wheelchair. I was stunned at her thoughtfulness, and in that moment, I was genuinely grateful that she had gone out of her way to create a more welcoming experience for my father. I gave her a smile and a nod, expressing my thanks. "Of course," she offered without hesitation, as if to acknowledge that this was likely not the only time I'd had to shoehorn my father and his wheelchair into a difficult space.

Unfortunately, when she attempted to begin her screening process, none of the diagnostic equipment could be used at dad's seated "height." We had to move the exam chair back into place and then get dad from his wheelchair into the exam chair. My father's medication was clearly starting to wear off, and it took more effort than usual to complete the transition. I pulled him up from his wheelchair to a standing position while facing me and then helped him rotate to the exam chair. We moved together until his backside was aligned with the chair, slowly shuffling through the world's most depressing waltz, punctuated with the soft thud of my father landing in the plastic-encased leather seat.

Because of his horrible posture, I had to prop my father up the same way I had earlier. Unfortunately, he was still having trouble keeping his eyes open. The doctor had to physically hold his eyelids open to complete the exam. This clearly was atypical, but the doctor was handling the situation with grace, poise, and professionalism. Her empathy was deeply reassuring and refreshing. I had become so used to supporting my father on my own, and I felt a surge of lightness having someone go even slightly out of their way to take a slice of the burden, if only for a moment.

Unfortunately, I was brought back down to earth somewhat abruptly. "It looks like we've done everything we can with corrective lenses," the doctor told us. "I'm concerned you might have glaucoma and cataracts, so you're going to have to see an ophthalmologist." With referral slip in hand, I wearily wheeled my dad back out to the lobby.

Considering that my father's current pair of glasses were being held around his head by a string (both ear rests were missing) and recognizing that I may need to replace them again soon, I picked out a couple of inexpensive plastic frames. As we were getting the new frames fitted, Dad was beginning to let me know that he desperately needed to get back to the nursing home.

"I need my pills," he told me. I could sense the fear in his voice.

I glanced at my cell phone to discover we had been away from the nursing home for almost two hours. "We're almost done, Dad. I promise."

The clerk was working methodically to adjust the new glasses, but my dad had had enough. "Just finish this up and let me get the hell out of here," he spat.

As I looked at him then and there, the helplessness consumed me. I wanted to get away from the feeling, but I couldn't. I had to take a deep breath and wait it out. Just as my dad was losing control of his world, I was losing control of the situation. I wanted so badly to help, but helping often meant discovering that there were just more problems ahead. It was daunting to walk out of that eye exam with the gut punch diagnosis of glaucoma and cataracts as well as the weight of yet another medical office visit looming. We were slowly plodding our way up a mountain, and every time we reached the what we thought was the peak, we realized another summit higher on the mountain was waiting for us.

"That'll be two-hundred seventy-eight dollars," said the clerk. "How would you like to pay?"

CHAPTER 15

BEARING WITNESS

———

In May of 2017, the head physician at the Hebrew Home recommended that my father be placed on hospice care. He had declined precipitously in the previous months, and I had known it was only a matter of time before this transition would come.

In the words of each of the professionals who administered occupational, speech, and physical therapy, my father had "plateaued." He was showing no improvement, and in some cases, he continued a downward slide away from the various goals and objectives that had been set for him. He had long since reached the point where he was "maxed out" on his daily dose of Sinemet, producing a one-two punch of unfortunate outcomes. Because of his growing tolerance for the medicine, each pill provided diminishing benefit. On top of that, as his physical condition continued to decline, he needed more of the medicine's effects just to operate. Though I had wished the deep brain stimulation procedure had produced a positive outcome for my father, we never saw a measurable benefit from the surgery, even after years living with the electrodes in place.

My father was fully bound to the wheelchair without exception. All essential daily functions required assistance from the staff at the Hebrew Home. We were both frustrated that he was no longer able to use the phone in his room to call me. Instead, when I picked up calls from him, I would hear the voice of the nurse on duty that night.

"Hi, Josh, this is Kaya. Your father wanted to speak to you," I would hear. There would be a rustling of the receiver, and then my father would speak in a breathy, muddled rasp. "Josh, where have you been?" he would say. "I need you here."

Perhaps the biggest issue was the deterioration of my father's cognitive state. My visits had gone from exchanging rants about Donald Trump and the New York Knicks to testing whether my father knew he was speaking to his oldest son. He was having trouble separating fact from fiction, and the timing of major events of his life were jumbled in his mind. He expressed worry that my mother was sleeping with an old friend of his. On more than one occasion, he asked me how my boyfriend was doing. I had never had a boyfriend, and my father by then had met Kate. For a period, he believed he was still in the sign business. He told me he just cut a deal with the Hebrew Home to replace the sign outside the building for $4,000. He would routinely ask if I had given them the drawings of the proposed new designs.

His vision had gotten steadily worse, and as much as I was pushing for my father to have cataract surgery to address the situation, his physician had advised against it. "There's not enough of a conscious brain to justify the procedure," he had told me. I was shocked by the way his assessment was worded, but I could not say I was surprised to hear it. This kind of validation signified my father had entered a stage in which corrective treatment was no longer reasonable. Like the stage of car ownership at which the cost of the needed repairs far outweighed the value of the vehicle, you simply drove until the engine stopped running.

On top of the severe vision impairment, he could no longer operate the television remote with his rigid and inflexible hands, making the appliance nearly obsolete. I would turn on the nightly news or a basketball game as I was leaving, hoping the sound would keep him company or provide some nominal entertainment. My father's cousin Mark had procured a device that played audiobooks, but I don't think I ever saw any of the tapes moved from the position I had left them in during my previous trip to the nursing home.

On one hand, I saw the transition to hospice as a form of giving up. On the other, much more practical hand, it was an acknowledgment of the objective reality of my father's current state. Hospice care was a good thing for him, and I reassured myself as I went through the intake documents. "Hospice care is primarily palliative rather than curative," they explained. "Palliative care means patient- and family-centered care that optimizes the quality of life by anticipating, preventing, and treating suffering." As I signed the forms, I couldn't help but think of the juxtaposition of my life against my father's. My existence as a runner had become one full of routine, intentional, and systematic exposure to suffering. Suffering well—suffering the right way—translated to strength and speed and most importantly, to endurance. My father's suffering had ceased to be productive many years prior. At that point, he needed comfort more than anything. And for him, I wasn't sure whether enduring any further was a good thing.

My visits became woefully challenging, but I resigned myself to continue seeing my father on a regular basis. I had come this far, and I wasn't going to stop showing up for my dad, even if he wasn't fully "there." If nothing else, my responsibility was to bear witness to his existence and remain a conduit to the world beyond the walls of the nursing home.

In early June, I entered room 520 of the Hebrew Home to find my father asleep in his wheelchair, without a shirt and leaning sharply to the side, one arm hanging straight down toward the carpet.

"Hey, Dad, I'm here," I said loudly to jolt him awake.

My father raised his head, and struggled to lift his eyelids. "Can you get me my water?" He asked in a low, hoarse voice.

I reached for the Styrofoam cup on the rolling table, marked with the day's date in pen. Next to the cup was an open packet of Hormel Thick & Easy instant food and beverage thickener. Because of his immense difficulty swallowing, he had been placed on a strict diet, requiring all of his food and drinks to retain the consistency of honey. That included his water.

I raised the cup to his chin, the clear plastic straw making contact with his lips. Without his vision, this was how I had to give him his cue to drink. He slowly opened his mouth to receive the straw and began taking in the liquid with deliberate, audible gulps.

"Thank you," he said. "What's new?"

"I just got back from a business trip to Eugene," I told him. "I was there for a few days for a conference at the University of Oregon. Managed to get a couple of early morning runs in along the Willamette River."

Within the span of a few sentences, though, my father had drifted back to sleep, his head slightly tilted to the side, mouth open wide.

"Let's get you a shirt," I said, moving over to the dresser. "It's almost time to for dinner, too," I told him, recognizing the hour on the wall clock. "We need to roll you over to the cafeteria."

A few minutes later, I was settling my dad at his spot within the cafeteria in front of a white paper placemat. Over the years, he had shared that spot at the table with a number of other residents, but now, he was the sole attendee. I pulled an arm chair over from its location along the wall and sat down next to him, lifting the large white disposable bib from beside his place setting and carefully tying it around his neck.

I fed my father for the first time nearly a decade earlier on December 21, 2008. It was his first day living at the Washington Center for Aging Services, the nursing home he was at for a few months right after moving out of St. Mary's and before transitioning to the Hebrew Home. I remembered that date distinctly because I had walked outside the nursing home and immediately started crying as I was unlocking my bike from the wrought iron fence along the edge of the property. Ten years later, I no longer felt scared, ashamed, or somber helping my dad eat. I didn't feel much of anything. It was part of our routine now, and I was continuing to do what I had always done for my dad. If there had been emotional soreness or sensitivity attached to this act, repetition had replaced those feelings with a thick callous.

I looked out across the cafeteria. A pair of gray-haired and bespectacled women shared the next table over, each appearing tiny against the backdrop of their wheelchairs. One of them kept repeating, "Excuse me," over and over in a shrill voice, looking wearily in the direction of the nurse who was working systematically to deliver trays to everyone in the room.

I recognized the man at the far end of the room, seated next to his walker, his head bobbing up and down and shaking side-to-side rhythmically. Jeffrey was another resident with Parkinson's, perhaps fifteen years my father's junior. I didn't know much of his story other than the fact that he had lived a few blocks away from where I had purchased a home with Kate in northeast DC a year prior. He looked back at me with a crooked smile.

My father's tray was set down by a young nurse named Holly wearing scrubs with cartoon animal prints. I lifted the maroon plastic dome from the plate to reveal a scoop of mashed potatoes, a dollop of pureed yams, and a small cylinder of meatloaf topped by a single stripe of ketchup. A shallow moat of light brown gravy surrounded the three smooth mounds of food, each topped by a few flecks of pepper. The consistency reminded me of the split pea soup at the Cranford Family Restaurant, a place my father used to take my brother and me after my parents separated and he didn't have groceries to cook dinner. I would order the Mickey Special—grilled cheese, French fries, and a cup of soup—off the kid's menu, which was printed on a paper placemat the server laid in front of me when I sat down in the booth.

I lifted the metal spoon from the table and dipped it into the mashed potatoes. I brought the spoon up to my father's mouth and gently pressed it against his lips. He pulled the potatoes into his mouth, closing his jaw deliberately, and loudly swallowed the texture-less material.

I couldn't imagine that the bite was fulfilling. I thought back to the hospice intake form and the line about "optimizing quality of life." I closed my eyes for a moment, took a breath, and then reached for another spoonful from the plate.

CHAPTER 16

AND THEN RELIEF

—

My eyes slowly peeled open at the sound of my cell phone vibrating on the nightstand. The room was still dark, and my head was heavy as I struggled to lift it off the pillow. It was too early for my six thirty alarm to be going off.

I sat up just enough to see the screen glowing against the darkness. The words "Hebrew Home of Greater Washington" were slowly scrolling across the screen. I reached over to pick up the phone and answer the call.

"Hello? This is Josh."

"This is Daphne, from the Hebrew Home. I'm very sorry, Josh, but your father has died."

Adrenaline shot through my body and I began to hear a soft ringing in my ears. I swallowed and inhaled slowly. "Okay," was all I could muster at first. "How did it happen?"

"He went to sleep last night, and early this morning, he drew his last breath," Daphne explained.

That was it? I thought. My father's departure from this world was both anticlimactic and elegant all at once. In my mind, I had expected that my father would suffer a spectacular, even theatrical, demise. Perhaps choking violently on a piece of baked chicken or a spoonful of pureed sweet potatoes, his arms flailing as he fell to the linoleum tiles of the fifth-floor cafeteria.

"Do you have a funeral home selected?" Daphne asked, bringing me back to the conversation.

"Yes, I'll be there soon," I said. "Thank you."

It was mechanical and scripted, just like the phone calls I had gotten when he fell or when he had been transported to the emergency room. I was about to hang up when I heard her speak again.

"I'm very sorry, Josh. You are a good son. And your dad loved you very much."

They were only a few words, but they were powerful. I wasn't looking for validation from the Five West charge nurse, but it meant the world to me. Daphne was the one who deserved the credit. She and her colleagues had supported my father for years.

"Thank you, Daphne. I appreciate everything you've done for my father."

I turned over to Kate who was still emerging from a deep sleep.

"Who was that?" she said, propping herself up on her elbow.

"My dad is dead."

"Oh, Josh, I'm so sorry!" she said, pressing her body into mine.

It hadn't hit me yet, but I knew it would. The moment was still abstract, like a fuzzy image slowly enhancing to better resolution. I had spent years anticipating this phone call, and it was over in a matter of seconds. This call was different from the rest, though. This call was the last I would receive from the nursing home. This call carried the last update on my father's condition I would ever get. This call brought everything to an end.

The predawn journey to Rockville felt unfamiliar, despite having made the trip so many times before. There was no urgency now, no anxiety about what kind of shape my father would be in that day. Instead, I felt relief. The weight of my father was gone: his chronic pain, his dulled cognition, his crooked back, his curled-up hands.

I looked over at Kate. She was gazing at me from the passenger seat with deep concern. She placed a hand on my shoulder and rubbed in circles. Seven weeks prior, we had gotten married in Prince William Forest Park on a beautiful, mild weekend in August. We were surrounded by 140 of our closest family members and friends as we read each other our vows. José Gonzalez's cover of "Heartbeats" played during the recessional. My father, however, was not there. I had made the difficult decision to leave him out, believing that his presence would detract from the focus of the day. Too many people hadn't seen him in a long time, and many had never met him before. To see him, or meet him, in that state would have been challenging and difficult for many of the guests.

And while I didn't necessarily want to protect anyone from the reality of my father's decline, putting him on display in that way wasn't a goal of the event. It was a day for me and Kate and those witnessing us to celebrate love and union. On top of that, I didn't believe my dad had more than a few minutes each hour when he was lucid enough to recognize his surroundings or communicate effectively. I further justified the decision by not wanting to remove him from the nursing home for the minimum of six or so hours it would have required, especially to an outdoor location without wheelchair accessibility. Kate and I had discussed a separate wedding ceremony we would perform in his room at the Hebrew Home so he could participate. Sadly, that would never happen.

I signed into the nursing home visitor log that morning at a quarter to six, and as I set the pen back down on the page, I felt the impulse to count the number of times I had visited. I had probably written my name in that book five hundred times in the previous nine years.

Arriving at the entrance to room 520, I saw my father's outline in bed. He was more still than I'd ever seen him. The sheets were pulled up to his chest, covering his thin, angular frame. His eyes and mouth were wide open, the same gaping stare he'd possessed when his consciousness would leave the room in the middle of our conversations. The look on his face was a reaction as if the world were simultaneously a wondrous spectacle and shockingly bewildering.

"It's okay, Dad. You did good. I've got it from here." Like so many times before, I leaned over to kiss him goodbye on the middle of his forehead.

Kate came up beside me, looking down forlornly at the father-in-law she never really had the chance to know before his mind began to wither so substantially. "I'm so sorry, Maury." She placed a hand against his cheek and temple.

Tears welled up in my eyes and started pouring down my face, though I wasn't mourning. The mourning had started long before. It had started when my father's dementia set in, when he could no longer feed himself, when he could no longer carry on a conversation. It had started when the Parkinson's diagnosis changed his life and forced him into a position of selfishness and fear, instantly de-prioritizing his role as a father. I cried because Kate was there, and she was there for me. In a caregiving journey dominated by feelings of loneliness, the final stretch had delivered me to a partner to whom I was immeasurably connected. My father had been with me for the entirety of my single life. Kate would be with me from that point forward.

I turned back to the door to my father's room and saw that a half a dozen members of the nursing staff on my father's floor had assembled to pay their respects. I hugged each of them, thanking them individually for the countless acts of service they had performed in support of my father. I had always stood in awe of their work, of their commitment to care. Far too often was it done without thanks and without recognition well outside of the view of others.

A few months prior, I had called a funeral home in Rockville to learn more about costs and logistics of a burial. I had discussed some options with one of the directors, including potentially transporting my father's body to New Jersey so he could be interred in Beth Israel Cemetery. His sister had purchased a plot there for her and my father right next to the resting place of their parents. However, I hated the idea that my father would lie in some sad, somber place; and that I would need to drag myself and my family there in perpetuity on the anniversary of his death or some other arbitrary date that happened to be convenient. I didn't want that. I wanted to bring my father's remains to a place where we shared joy. It had to be a place that made me smile, and that I knew would make him smile. I hadn't made up my mind where that was, but I knew it would be my decision. I also decided he would be cremated, so I could choose that place when I was ready.

I called the twenty-four-hour hotline for the funeral home, and within twenty minutes, a white man in his early forties with thinning hair arrived with a plain-looking gurney in tow. He asked me to leave the room so he could prep my father's body for transport.

"Someone will be in touch later today with next steps," he said, wheeling the gurney out of the room. "Again, I'm very sorry for your loss."

Later that day, I went for a run in Rock Creek Park. The sky was overcast, and as soon as I stepped on the trail, I felt the first few drops of rain on my shoulders. I wound my way over the Western Ridge and Valley Trails, communing with the dirt and trees that had given me purpose and refuge for so many miles and years. The rain became heavier and heavier, and I pushed on, desperate for the space to think. I reflected on the nature of fragility and the value of caring for myself. I thought about gratitude and the privilege of getting to push my body over long distances. I pulled my phone out of my armband and opened up the voice memos app to start a new recording as I continued running along the trail.

"When you're young," I spoke into the device, "you are restless because you don't know a lot. When you get a little bit older, maybe you get a little bit too cautious because you've had to grapple with the realities of the world. The key," I explained, coaching and consoling myself, "is to settle somewhere in the middle after recognizing our own assets and our own elasticity, and then position ourselves for a personalized version of success."

In the early evening, we stopped by my father's cousin Mark's house. Years earlier, I had asked Mark to store the bulk of my father's art collection since I had no space in the room I was renting at the time. After getting the stacks of pastel, charcoal, and watercolor pieces home, Kate and I began to go through them, one by one. We found a series of dozens of drawings of scantily clad women in various positions, and in many of those works, we also saw a thin vertical line. After a few minutes of leafing through the sketches, I realized what I was actually looking at. These were quite clearly drawings of strippers. My father had drawn these at Camelot, the strip club on M Street. He had been telling the truth about why he was there when I confronted him with his cell phone. I was shocked and tickled, all at once. "I stand corrected," I said aloud, a smile forming on my face as I shook my head back and forth in disbelief.

I made the decision to have two memorials: one in Washington, DC and one in New Jersey. On the day of the memorial in DC, friends, relatives, colleagues, and neighbors crowded into the ground floor of our tiny rowhouse. Kate and I had taken dozens of my father's artworks and tacked them up on the dining room wall. Several portraits, a still life of fruit, a number of lush landscapes, a canal-side village, and a half dozen nude subjects, including a few of the sketches of strippers.

At a time that felt as good as any, I planted myself in the corner of the house and began to address those gathered. "Maury Lasky was a good man, and I will remember him that way. He was a loving father and friend, sometimes successful entrepreneur, teller of jokes, roller disco enthusiast, dedicated artist and sculptor, traveler, and triathlete. He was known for his infectious smile, his amazing sense of humor, his stubbornness, his confidence, and his keen ability to judge character. He was, like all of us, flawed. My father made mistakes, some of which I'll never forgive him for. But those mistakes also made him the person he was.

"My father was a great dad to me and my brother when he was healthy. He went all out when it came to our birthday parties. When I was five or six, he dressed up in a homemade Teenage Mutant Ninja Turtles costume. I remember freaking out, though, because it wasn't the most convincing disguise, and I could still tell it was him. But I know, deep down, those were tears of love since I knew just how much he adored me. He also came up with my Bar Mitzvah theme, the 'Art of Being Josh,' for which he superimposed my face on famous paintings. It was a tedious process that started with a photo shoot, during which he had me pose in the same orientation as the subjects in the *Mona Lisa*, *The Scream*, *Sleeping Gypsy*, and many more. Then he scaled and printed the photos and cut them out using an X-Acto knife, pasting them onto copies of the various works. Those became table centerpieces at the Martinsville Inn that Saturday afternoon.

"Even when he was sick, my father taught me lessons. Despite becoming increasingly limited in his physical capabilities, he always believed that anything was possible. When he was living at St. Mary's Court, he decided to dress up as the Incredible Hulk for the annual Halloween party. I told him I would meet him there for the party, but he wasn't in the lobby with the other residents when I got to the building. After about twenty minutes, though, my father emerged from the elevator covered head to toe in green paint. Green acrylic paint. It was absurd, to say the least.

"I will continue to hold on to two pieces of clothing that belonged to my dad because they make me smile. The first is a t-shirt he wore right up until the last days of his life. I don't know whether he himself thought it was funny to wear it or whether the nurses at the Hebrew Home put it on him as a joke, but I love it either way. The front of the t-shirt says, 'North Shore Care Supply: The Incontinence Supply Experts.' The back of the shirt says, 'Yes, there is a better way!' The other piece of clothing is a t-shirt that shows my dad's pride in his physical appearance, even after he started to become thin and wiry. When he was living at St. Mary's

Court, I found him walking around Foggy Bottom, with his walker, wearing what used to be a collared shirt. Except, the collar had been roughly trimmed off, along with each of the sleeves and the bottom half of the torso, so when he wore it, his midriff was exposed."

My tone shifted slightly as I entered more serious territory. I wanted to share some of the lessons my father had imparted on me, and I wanted to tie a thread between the artwork in the room and the nature of expression, particularly my effort to tell my father's story.

"Though he was an artist his whole life, my father turned to art as a refuge to cope with his Parkinson's. And, just as he struggled with his art, which you can see in his tense, anxious scribbles, so too did I toil and suffer with telling his story. Our story. He suffered, as I did and as I do, as an artist. In the same way each of us endures pain as artists of various kinds, using different mediums.

"I arrived at this notion that artists, in their suffering, deal with three types of pain. The first is the pain of experience. This is the pain of trauma and life's unfairness. Everyone deals with shitty circumstances. No one is immune, and no one has a perfect existence. Life produces pain and suffering for us, and we are forced to cope.

"The second is the pain of expression. This is the pain that comes with the inability to attach accurate labels to things we observe in the world or to translate what we see through charcoal and pastel to a drawing or from words and sentences to a story. It is also the pain that comes with the reality that nothing in our world is black and white. There are no absolutes, only gray areas. And this, at best, renders expression a frustrating exercise.

"The last is the pain of iteration. This is the pain that comes with the realization that nothing final is truly final. That there is no perfect. That there is only the latest in a line of versions that will never actually end. I see that very clearly in my father's art. There are multiple versions of the same work, and sometimes, there are lines on top of lines on top of lines within the same piece. My father, for example, struggled with drawing faces, and you can see that the paper is almost worn through at the faces of some of his subjects with erasures and the retreading of his pen.

"But with the pain of iteration comes a kind of liberation. For in our endless versions of things, we realize that we are incapable of the perfect version, and no final form is required of us. We are free to create and recreate, to tell and retell as we feel compelled to do so. That is our human right, and our gift."

***

Two weeks later, Kate and I drove up to New Jersey for the second of the two memorials, this one held at my mother's house—my childhood home and the home my parents had raised me in—for those who lived close by. On the day of the memorial, I saw people I hadn't seen since I was a teenager. Extended family members, my parents' friends, the grown-up versions of children I knew long ago. My aunt's first ex-husband, Mel, someone I only really knew from pictures and stories, showed up. There were even divorced couples who were back in the same room for the first time. I smiled recognizing that my father had a special way of bringing people together.

I took my place again at the corner of the room to speak, but my eulogy was slightly different this time. I held a grudge against a number of these people who didn't bother to show up for my dad in the way I had hoped. Somehow, however, they had found their way to his memorial service. I appreciated their presence, without a doubt, but I would have appreciated it more if it wasn't the first time I had seen some of them in a decade or more.

"It is infinitely easier to visit someone in health than it is to visit them in sickness," I explained. "It is terrible when we must come face to face with the reality of the wrath of age, decline, and disability, and what that does to the people we love. We have to recognize that people don't exist as we once knew them. They exist as they are now. And it's not fair to abandon the people we love just because it's difficult or frustrating or depressing to witness them as they are, even if they appear as less than we thought them to be."

People around the room shifted uncomfortably. Eyes began looking toward the ground. A few people kept their eyes on mine and nodded as I spoke. My message was delivered. It was arguably the most powerful piece of feedback I had ever given in my life. And I hope it encouraged at least one person to do one thing they might not have done before. That would have made me happy.

As people started to depart the house, I found a moment of quiet to myself. I turned to the collage of my father's art I had recreated on the wall, this time in my mother's living room, and fixated on a single watercolor. A tall expressionless brunette woman in a bright red bathing suit stood cross-legged on the sand of a beach beneath a clear blue sky. Her head was pointed in the direction of the ocean, a single wave beginning to break toward the shore. In the background, two figures held hands as they walked together toward the water.

CHAPTER 17

CLAY, SILT, AND SAND

On Friday, April 26, 2019, Kate and I boarded Southwest Flight 1096 from Baltimore-Washington International to Phoenix Sky Harbor. My backpack was heavier than normal, as I was toting an extra bottle of water so I could hydrate during the plane ride. It was a necessary measure, as the next day, I was hoping to cover forty-nine miles through the hottest, driest, and highest altitude conditions I had ever run in.

Shortly after my father's death, I found myself routinely returning to the same feeling I had when I was recovering from my broken ankle. It was a deep desire not to take anything for granted, to push myself further, to explore my maximum potential. In the words of Thoreau, "I wanted to live deep and suck out all the marrow of life." I turned, yet again, to ultrarunning as a vehicle to get me to that marrow. Several years prior, one particular run had caught my attention just as I was beginning to push myself beyond marathon distance. Outside of competing in a hundred-miler, nearly every ultrarunner gives some thought to a double crossing of the Grand Canyon, known as Rim to Rim to Rim. For many it's a bucket list item. The combination of distance, climbing, gorgeous scenery, and required self-reliance admittedly appealed to me, and I began doing research. I had also decided to stop waiting, and to set a date to attempt the run at the earliest opportunity.

Three months prior, Kate and I had traveled to Tanzania for our honeymoon. She advocated for the safari and the beaches of Zanzibar, and I had suggested adding a hike of Kilimanjaro to our itinerary. Kate dutifully obliged, and despite intense headaches and pervasive gastrointestinal distress, we managed to drag ourselves to the summit at the end of a seven-day trek. It was a test of endurance, sure, but it hadn't required physical conditioning as much as it did mental toughness and a willingness to suffer through pain. The challenge also required us to lean on each other, to communicate through discomfort, and to be okay receiving help. We were supported every step of the way by guides, porters, and a cook. It was a bit of a tease, though, as well. Hiking uphill for a week made me yearn for running. On the next to last day of the trip, I ran three miles along Nungwi Beach in northern Zanzibar in bare feet. That was the first workout of an eleven-week training period that led up to my trip to Arizona, during which I had managed to pack in eight races that started with a half marathon and ramped up to a muddy reprise of the Bull Run Run 50-Miler.

We spent the three-hour drive north from Phoenix listening to Malcolm Gladwell's *Revisionist History* podcast, in which he presents an alternative view of popular events and cultural phenomenon. In the seventh episode of the first season, he begins by talking about Elvis Costello's song "The Deportee's Club" off the album *Goodbye Cruel World*. The fast-paced and overproduced track, released in 1984, is almost universally accepted as awful listening. But a full decade later, Elvis recorded the album for a re-release that included a completely new version of the song, stripped down to only vocals and an acoustic guitar, immaculate in its new sound. Gladwell argues that, sometimes, creativity takes time and iteration.

He makes a similar argument about "Hallelujah." The song was originally produced by Leonard Cohen, who tortured himself to craft the track, spending five years and writing some fifty different verses for the song. Cohen eventually recorded the song in 1984 to very little critical acclaim. In 1991, artist John Cale recorded a cover of the song for an obscure Leonard Cohen tribute album called *I'm Your Fan* on a tiny French music label. A few years later, the then unknown Jeff Buckley recorded his cover of "Hallelujah" in 1994 on the album *Grace*—again to very little critical acclaim. It was only after his tragic death in 1997 that Buckley's version, a cover of John Cale's version, became a well-known work of art. Since then, it has been covered by hundreds of artists, each providing their own unique reproduction.[4]

Since his death, I continued to struggle with the story of my father's life. During the years I cared for my dad, I turned to writing quite often, typing out exasperated journal entries that offered the utility of allowing me to vent. The stories weren't particularly good, but the sequence of events was there, along with my observations and my feelings. I would set the stories aside and then come back to revisit them after months or years. Each time, I was suddenly viewing both the written material and my memories in a completely new light. I was older, more experienced, and possessed new and greater perspectives. I had changed, and so had the story.

---

4   Malcolm Gladwell, "Hallelujah," July 28, 2016, *Revisionist History*, produced by Panoply Media, podcast, MP3 audio, 40:21.

I began to realize that all stories go through a transformation over time. They age in the same way a mature tomato plant does; the plant becomes wildly efficient, shedding unnecessary leaves and twisting its vines in a way that sends as much water and nutrients to its fruit. The plant emphasizes its best parts, laden with its own seed, in an attempt to extend an echo of itself beyond the end of its own life. I also began to realize that at some point, it is more important to tell a story than to wait for age to improve it. There was relief in telling a story, both for the teller who gets to transmit a narrative and also for an audience who may take part in that narrative secondhand and add validity to the teller by bearing witness.

We arrived at the Grand Hotel just after sunset, an ember glow emanating from the distant horizon behind the building. Stepping out of the car, I could see nearly the full extent of Tusayan, a tiny town of hotels and restaurants nestled a few miles away from the Grand Canyon's South Rim. For dinner, we walked across State Route 64 to Plaza Bonita where we split a pitcher of margaritas and gorged on chimichangas and enchiladas. After dinner, I laid out the gear, food, and water I would need for the run and then got into bed to get as much rest as possible.

At three in the morning, the marimba tune of my iPhone alarm began blaring inches from my ear. After brushing my teeth, I called a twenty-four-hour cab service and asked for a pickup in fifteen minutes. Leaving Kate fast asleep, I zipped up my running pack and headed outside to meet my ride. Twenty minutes later, I was stepping out the door of the van into the South Kaibab trailhead parking lot. A single overhead streetlight was the only source of illumination as far as my eyes could see, and the only sound I could detect was the rustling of wind in the sagebrush that lined the path to the rim of the canyon. I could tell there was an edge there, but it remained undefined somewhere in the blackness ahead. Instantly, I was reminded of the psychological power of darkness to inspire loneliness and trepidation. I flicked on my headlamp and rubbed my arms to generate a bit of warmth in the forty-seven-degree coolness.

A moment later, I heard another van pulling down the drive to the parking lot. Out spilled a woman and a man, each in their forties or fifties, with athletic builds and the minimal gear I'd expect to see from seasoned runners. They greeted me with a nod and a smile as they approached the start of the trail, chatting about the conditions they expected down below.

Without much hesitation, I recognized the opportunity before me. "Do you mind if I run with guys for a little bit?" I asked with a slight hint of desperation in my tone.

"Not at all! Please do," the woman responded with more enthusiasm than I could imagine anyone mustering at a quarter to four in the morning.

I stuck with Jessica and Casey as we descended the switchbacks of the South Kaibab Trail, only getting my first good look at their faces nearly two hours and six miles later as we crossed the Black Bridge over the Colorado River with the beginnings of daylight. They were veteran mountain ultrarunners with multiple hundred-milers under their belts. Casey was preparing for Western States, the Super Bowl of ultradistance races, and Rim to Rim to Rim was part of his training. We exchanged stories about races as the canyon walls began to glow an ever-deeper shade of red with the rising sun.

We refilled our water at Phantom Ranch, one of two sources of potable water on the route, and continued on the

North Kaibab trail toward the North Rim. The temperature was climbing into the eighties by mid-morning, and the terrain became steeper and steeper. The scrubby desert vegetation gave way to rocks as the inclined trail became a series of switchbacks up to the rim. The higher we climbed, the more massive the canyon stretched out around us.

To my surprise, there were patches of snow along the highest parts of the North Rim trail, and the trailhead itself, still closed for the season, was covered in a layer of snow. After a short rest, we turned and headed back down toward the canyon floor. I descended quickly, rolling effortlessly with the trail back to Manzanita Rest House, stopping there to refill my bottles and change out my socks. After thirty-one miles, my body was feeling as well as I could expect.

Unfortunately, the next eight miles were difficult, as my legs became heavy and my head started to pound. I was dragging as we made it back to Phantom Ranch, and the sugar of the cafeteria's signature lemonade didn't lift me to a better state. The heat was brutal as we pushed forward, and my exhaustion was amplified by cramping in my quads and calves. We crossed Silver Bridge to begin the final ten miles of the run, a four-thousand-foot ascent back to the South Rim.

The initial climb out of the canyon was slow and painful. I recognized that I may have gone a bit too hard coming down from the North Rim, and I had slacked on my calorie intake toward the middle of the day. At one point, I took off my pack and lay down in a stream, fully submerging myself in the cool flowing water. It did absolutely nothing to make me feel better. My temples were throbbing, and my insides felt hollow.

In that low place, I thought about my father. I decided that my next adventure would be the telling of our story. I would finish the book I had started writing in frustrated rants to no one in particular after nights spent in a hospital emergency room or waiting for the Metro late into the evening after a visit to the nursing home.

I got out of the stream, soaking wet, and turned back to the trail. With a nod to Jessica and Casey, I started a light jog. My body had quit, so it was time for my mind to take over. I willed myself to push through the heat and pain for those final six miles.

As I was coming up the final few hundred yards of the Bright Angel trail, I could feel the emotions welling up from deep within me. That moment, and the moment right before the end of any race, run, or ride, was always the most vivid in my mind. I knew the finish was imminent, and I felt torn between the will to complete the effort and my reluctance to let go of it. It was a moment of paradox, of polar opposites attempting to coexist. They formed a beautiful balance in my mind, a tension that couldn't quite be resolved until I got back to that place during the final moments of the next adventure. In contrast, a life is not like a race, run, or ride with a discrete and known finish. There was no moment just before the end of my father's life to recognize and savor and celebrate. There were, however, plenty of moments well before the end, before hospice and dementia and wheelchairs, that I had worked hard to make count for all they were worth.

I leaned into the ascent, planting my trekking poles in the red-orange dirt and willing myself up the incline. Turning the last switchback, I looked up to the lip of the canyon to see the most beautiful smile in the world on Kate's face.

***

Six months later, on Friday, October 4, Kate and I were driving north on I-95 to spend a few days in New Jersey. We had loaded the trunk with the things we'd typically bring on a weekend away from our home in DC. There were, however, two notable additions to our cargo: a shovel and the wooden box containing my father's remains.

I had been looking at the box on a shelf in my bedroom for close to a year. Though I had the idea almost immediately after he died, I had wanted to wait before committing my father's ashes to a final resting place. With time, I became certain he belonged at Second Avenue in Bradley Beach. It was the only place that made sense. I didn't want a gravestone or a plot. I didn't want perpetual visits to a gated, grassy, gloomy patch of land. Only the happy memories of sun, sand, waves, and warmth. Only that place I knew we both loved.

The next day, Kate and I walked together, surrounded by my mother, my brother, and a few close friends to the entrance to Second Avenue Beach. We walked past the dunes and toward the water's edge, the low tide waves lapping at the shore. I found a place that might have been a great spot during a crowded day in the summer, close enough to the ocean to guarantee a breeze but not close enough for a big wave to come along and soak your stuff. Then, I began to dig. After a few minutes, I passed the shovel to my brother, and then to Kate, then to my mother, and to the others who were there. We dug the kind of hole my father would be proud of.

I stepped down a few feet into the space. It possessed a serene quality, slightly quieter than up above. As I stood there, I thought about my father, just as I had at the bottom of the Grand Canyon. I thought about the lows he endured with depression back when I was a child and my parents were together. I thought about the steep uphill climbs he looked at every day with Parkinson's, just getting out of bed, putting on his clothes, and brushing his teeth. I thought about the end of his life, when his body itself had become an unscalable canyon, and he remained trapped within, fully dependent on others to move and do and be. And yet, he persisted. At some point, the walls get too deep to even recognize as walls because there's no more light coming in through the opening at the top. Or worse, your mind has completely lost touch with the concept of up or down or movement. It hurt me deep in my gut to think that that's how my father's journey ended.

In that moment, I remembered that even the ability to recognize the walls of a canyon around you is a beautiful thing. And if you're lucky enough to have it, the ability to pull yourself out of that canyon is even more beautiful. The depths remind us of the value of gratitude. Without constraints, we cannot appreciate freedom. Without struggle, we cannot appreciate ease. My mind went back to the moment I encountered that tunnel in West Virginia on my bike. I thought about pedaling into the hollow darkness, about the fear and uncertainty, and how it gave way to renewed strength, resolve, and light.

I took the knife from my pocket—the same knife I carried with me as I biked across the country—and cut a small slit in the corner of the plastic bag that contained my father's ashes.

"Goodbye, Dad," I said quietly, the tears forming lines down my cheeks as I turned the bag over.

I looked up to see Kate and Max offering me their hands. With their help, I stepped up and embraced them and the others one by one. I filled in the hole, smoothing the top with the edge of the shovel. As we left that spot, I looked back over my shoulder toward the edge of the water, looking forward to the next time I'd return. Perhaps for a run. Perhaps to dig another hole. Perhaps just to sit and be grateful.

APPENDIX

PROLOGUE

Family Caregiver Alliance. "Caregiver Statistics: Demographics." Last modified April 17, 2019. https://www.caregiver.org/caregiver-statistics-demographics.

National Alliance for Caregiving and AARP Family Caregiving. *Caregiving in the US* 2020. May 2020. Accessed May 4, 2020. https://www.aarp.org/content/dam/aarp/ppi/2020/05/full-report-caregiving-in-the-united-states.doi.10.26419-2Fppi.00103.001.pdf.

CHAPTER 12

McCarthy, Cormac. *The Road*. New York: Alfred A. Knopf, 2006.

CHAPTER 17

Gladwell, Malcolm. "Hallelujah." July 28, 2016. *Revisionist History*. Produced by Panoply Media. Podcast, MP3 audio, 40:21. http://revisionisthistory.com/episodes/07-hallelujah.

ACKNOWLEDGMENTS

This book would not have been possible without the love and support of the many people I am lucky to call family and friends. To you, I am forever grateful.

I must start with the many individuals who provided care to my father when he couldn't get by on his own. Thank you, Margaret Pully and the staff at St. Mary's Court as well as the incredible team of nurses, therapists, social workers, and doctors at the Hebrew Home of Greater Washington. I must also thank my cousins, Jeff Spieler and Mark Grisar, who showed up and helped out in ways that made a big difference for my father and for me. Thank you to my Aunt Eileen who made sacrifices to give my father a place to live for years before I moved him to Washington, DC.

I need to thank my life partner and best friend, Kate McMahon, for giving me the time and emotional support I needed to relive my experience and tell my story. Her generosity in allowing me the space to write this book is multiplied a thousand-fold by the fact that she was pregnant with our first child and there was a global pandemic during the nine months I worked on this project. Kate is, and will forever be, my personal hero.

Thank you to my mother, Susan Cohen Lasky, and my brother, Maxwell Lasky, for their lifelong unconditional love and support, and specifically during my time as a caregiver and throughout my journey to publish this book.

I must also thank the many individuals who helped me through some of the toughest, darkest moments of my journey as a caregiver. Those people include Ben Spears, Ben Varquez, Bernard Demczuk, Bonnie Kudwitt, Brian Hamluk, Carly Mercer, Chris Brooks, Chris Burke, Chris O'Brien, Corey Barenbrugge, Daniel Paschall, DJ Saul, Eric Grand, Erik Mendoza-Wilkenfeld, Garland Middleton, Gary Kudwitt, Geoff Grand, Jacqueline Hackett, John Bacon, John Sygielski, Kate Harkin, Kyle Compton, Linda Donnels, Lynn Grand, Megan Cronin, Michael Akin, Peter Konwerski, Renee Edelman, Roger Lowenstein, Scott Mory, Stephen Joel Trachtenberg, and Tim Miller. I should have done more to acknowledge you then. I am forever in your debt.

I also want to thank the very generous group of individuals that purchased a copy of this book during the pre-sale. You are the ones that made the publication of this story possible. Thank you for making an investment in my story and my writing. This group includes: Alex Pierre, Alexandra Rumschlag, Alicia Knight, Allison Bell Friedman, Amy Dong, Andrea Kuchli, Anthony Shop, Ashley Alvator Friedman, Alex Stoicof, Audrey Kruse, Barbara Sullivan, Bernard Demczuk, Ben Varquez, Benjamin Fuller, Beth Baum, Beth Stein, Blaine Collison, Bonnie Kudwitt, Brandon Posivak, Brendan Shane, Caridad Rodriguez, Carly Mercer, Carol Alvator, Carole Lambert, Carrie Warick-Smith, Casey Studhalter, Charles DeFanti, Cheryl Fiske, Chris Burke, Chris O'Brien, Cindy Stagoff, Claire & Garland Jeffreys, Corey Barenbrugge, Coy McKinney, Debbie Sullivan, Dallas Cruz, Dan Dzombak,

Dave Hirsch, David Escobar, David Holroyd, Deborah Crain Kemp, Debra McLaughlin, Devin Veca, Dave Wright, Diane D'Alessandro, DJ Saul, Dave Earl, Elizabeth Shope, Elizabeth Bontrager, Ella Greenberg, Emily Riordan, Eric Friedman, Erik Mendoza, Ernest Chrappah, Fiona Conroy, Gabe Klein, Ben Spears, Hanna Grene, Hannah Hickman, Hannah Debelius, Harrison Kudwitt, Hannah Grisar, Heather Kangas, Harry Ingram, Jamal Holtz, James Kuster, Jayne Mooney, Jeanne Braha, Jeff Henoch, Jeff Spieler, Jenee Gaynor, Jennifer Withrow, Jenny Wiedower, Jessie LaPointe, Justin Grand, Jim Core, Jodi Feldstein, Joe Nelson, Joe Bondi, John Giannico, Jonathan Cohen, Joshua Kaplan, Julia Craighill, Julie Ann Powasnik, Julie Skodowski, Justin George, Karen Galvin, Katherine Suell, Katie Harris, Krista Slosburg, Lauren McMahon, Lauren Weissman-Falk, Laurie Gama, Lina Musayev, Linda Weiss, Matt Lindsay, Lisa Bateman, Maggie Desmond, Marc Ciagne, Margaret Bruns, Margaret Hoffman, Margaret Pully, Margisel Adams, Maria Sonntag, Mark Coley, Mark Grisar, Mary Ellen Engel, Marybeth Young, Mason Sell, Matt Silverman, Megan Cronin, Michael Akin, Michael Polkowitz, Mindy Lissner, Maxwell Lasky, Mohammed Ali, Molly Mitzner, Nancy Lubarsky, Nathaniel Allen, Nicole Roberge, Oksana Balytsky, Pamela Gadinsky, Patrick Kirby, Patty Rose, Peter Loge, Philip Glatfelter, Phyllis Jacobs, Rebecca Nemec, Richard Livingstone, Rick Fedrizzi, Robert Argen, Robert Platt, Roger Lowenstein, Ronald Scheff, Ronnie Lissner, Russell Howd, Sam Chaleff, Scott Breen, Scott Mory, Seth Weinshel, Sheena Pegarido, Sherry Rutherford, Sora Kim, Stef Work, Steve Beam, Steve Ricken, Steve Rosenfield, Susan Cohen Lasky, Susan Maffei, Susan Mendelson, Susan Ebner, Suzanne Graves, Shannon Bishop-Green, Thomas Moserowitz, Tim Gowa, Tim Miley, Tim Miller, Tina Miller,

Toby Davidow, Tommy Galloway, Wanda Dunaway, William Dujardin, William Falk, Zach Dobelbower, and many others who chose to remain anonymous.

I must thank the team at New Degree Press for their hard work to support me on my publishing journey, including Julie Colvin, Amanda Brown, Anne Kelley, Brian Bies, Leila Summers, and Casey Mahalik. I also need to thank Eric Koester of the Creator Institute and Georgetown University for his encouragement and coaching. I also spoke to a number of individuals as I was writing this book, many of whom shared direct and candid insights about living with Parkinson's disease or supporting a family member with Parkinson's. Thank you to Beth Baum, Dominic Grossman, David La Couteur, Mike Moyer, and Riva Neam.

Made in the USA
Middletown, DE
06 June 2021

At Issue

Should Music Lyrics
Be Censored?

Other Books in the At Issue Series:

Are Americans Overmedicated?

Are Newspapers Becoming Extinct?

Are Social Networking Sites Harmful?

Casualties of War

Concealed Weapons

Corporate Corruption

Drunk Driving

The Ethics of Capital Punishment

Food Safety

How Can the Poor Be Helped?

Human Embryo Experimentation

Is Organic Food Better?

Is Socialism Harmful?

Media Bias

Sexting

Should Junk Food Be Sold in Schools?

Should Juveniles Be Given Life Without Parole?

Should Religious Symbols Be Allowed on Public Land?

Should the United States Be Multilingual?

Should There Be an International Climate Treaty?

At Issue

Should Music Lyrics Be Censored?

Beth Rosenthal, Book Editor

GREENHAVEN PRESS
A part of Gale, Cengage Learning

GALE
CENGAGE Learning

Detroit • New York • San Francisco • New Haven, Conn • Waterville, Maine • London

10. Explicit Lyrics Do Not Encourage Teen Sex   67
    Carla Stokes, interviewed by Bonnie Zylbergold

11. Rap and Hip-Hop Music Promote Violence   73
    Geoff Schumacher

12. Rap and Hip-Hop Music Reveal but Do Not   78
    Promote Violence
    Yan Dominic Searcy

13. Racist and Sexist Rap Lyrics Must Be Rejected   83
    by African Americans
    Anthony Asadullah Samad

14. Consumers of All Races Should Boycott   88
    Offensive Rap Music
    Justin D. Ross

15. Music Censorship Threatens Cultural Growth   92
    and Survival in Somalia
    Jessica Saxton

Organizations to Contact   97

Bibliography   102

Index   106

Introduction

Music, like many things, is highly subjective. Lyrics that some regard as thought-provoking and edgy might sound extremely hateful to others. What some people might find offensive and insulting, others will find to be relevant and meaningful. At what point does something cross the line and become a threat to others? At what point, if any, should people be limited as to what they can say or sing publicly? While the First Amendment states in part that "Congress shall make no law . . . abridging the freedom of speech," this has proven challenging in practice. Debate continues over how to protect the right to freedom of speech while respecting the rights of those who may be offended by that speech.

Can a musician be accused of inciting violence with the lyrics in a song? Gene Policinski, the First Amendment Center's senior vice president and executive director, talks about the case of Marc Hall, a soldier stationed at Fort Stewart, Georgia, who was arrested for writing a hip-hop song that criticizes the military and describes a shooting spree. Writing on the center's website on January 17, 2010, Policinski declared: "No one wants to be in the position of ignoring a potential threat that is later linked with a killing spree. But we should also be concerned that even speech that many find offensive may also be speech that gives voice to real concerns and that speaks to real issues—and that from the beginning of our nation we have restrained the power of government to silence those voices."

In 1985, Tipper Gore, the now-estranged wife of former vice president Al Gore, was inspired to found the Parents Music Resource Center (PMRC) after she listened to "Darling Nikki," a song by Prince that included references to sex and masturbation. A congressional committee heard testimony about the need for possible government regulation of lyrics. The Recording Industry Association of America (RIAA) began a parental advisory program that same year, in which recording companies voluntarily put warning labels on albums to alert parents to lyrics that might not be appropriate for children.

In her 1987 book *Raising PG Kids in an X-Rated Society*, Gore writes about the difficulty of striking a balance between protecting children and protecting free speech:

> Censorship is not the answer. In the long run, our only hope is for more information and awareness, so that citizens and communities can fight back against market exploitation and find practical means for restoring individual choice and control. As parents and as consumers, we have the right and the power to pressure the entertainment industry to respond to our needs. Americans, after all, should insist that every corporate giant—whether it produces chemicals or records—accept responsibility for what it produces.

In 1985, the list of the "Filthy Fifteen" artists who were cited for being among the most offensive included Prince, Judas Priest, AC/DC, Madonna, and Def Leppard. While the artists on the list have changed over the years, the controversy at the heart of the matter still remains the same: how far is too far? How much is too much? In discussing Russell Simmons's 2007 call for musicians to voluntarily refuse to use certain hateful terms, Sarah Rodman, in "Policing Rap Lyrics Is Near-Impossible Task" in the *Boston Globe*, April 25, 2007, asked, "But if we start arbitrarily outlawing certain words, where do we stop? Who gets sworn in to stand word patrol? And who gets penalized?"

Technology that makes it easy for children to access music and videos makes it even more difficult to balance free speech and protecting children from objectionable language and behavior. Rebecca Hagelin, writing in an August 17, 2010, column on Townhall.com, notes that "the industry excels at promoting across every platform available, especially video. Nearly every major pop star produces pornographic music videos

and pushes them to your children through Facebook fan pages
... and YouTube videos, plus MTV."

Along with the debate over whether music lyrics should be
censored, other related arguments persist as well: Can lyrics
that some find offensive be used to teach and reach kids?
What is the effect of censorship of any type on society? Do
some lyrics degrade women and encourage teens to have sex?
Are hip-hop and rap treated unfairly and wrongfully blamed
for problems in society? In the viewpoints presented in *At Issue: Should Music Lyrics Be Censored?* the authors debate the
effects of censorship on music in particular and society in
general.

Hip-Hop and Rap Lyrics Can Be Useful Teaching Tools

Mary Ellen Flannery

Mary Ellen Flannery is a senior writer and editor at the National Education Association.

There is a great tendency among educators to view hip-hop and rap music in only negative terms. Rather than causing young people to be violent and sexually active, rap and hip-hop can be used to reach children and to encourage them to learn. The lyrics and views found in hip-hip and rap music can put themes in contexts that children can easily understand, and to which they can relate. Simply put, hip-hip and rap allow teachers to communicate more easily with their students.

> "Yeah, this album is dedicated to all the teachers that told me I'd never amount to nothin', to all the people that lived above the buildings that I was hustlin' in front of that called the police on me when I was just tryin' to make some money to feed my daughters, and all the n-----s in the struggle—you know what I'm sayin'?"
>
> —*The Notorious B.I.G.*

Ooooh! Did he just say the N-word?

He did. And that's just one of the reasons that many educators give a little, "eh, I just don't think so," when it comes to

Mary Ellen Flannery, "Yo! From Tupac to the Bard," *NEA Today*, vol. 27, no. 3, November/December 2008, pp. 35–37. Copyright © 2008 by Mary Ellen Flannery. All rights reserved. Reproduced by permission of National Education Association.

using hiphop in the classroom. Much of it is profane or violent, offensive to women and gays, and just ... dangerous. Ugh. And you see the kids listening, rapt, heads bobbing, like some kind of genius prophet is speaking through those ear buds.

Just think: what's it doing to them?

Well, engaging them, for one thing.

These days, you can't turn the dial without tuning into chart-topping, millionaire hip-hop artists like 50 Cent or Ludacris, rapping street-smart about diamonds and drugs, poverty, and police brutality. (Sings Kanye West: "They say, 'Oh you graduated?' No, I decided I was finished chasing y'all dreams.") While you might immediately move on, muttering, "This is the new American jazz?" many of your students hear something that they believe speaks directly to them. Like it or not, over the past 20 years, hiphop has become key to the canon of contemporary music.

Wouldn't it be nice if they listened to you with the same attention? Or if they could quote Langston Hughes with the same fluency? Well, consider this: Many of your colleagues believe it's possible, even paramount, to use hip-hop to build exactly those kinds of connections.

While you might immediately move on, muttering, "This is the new American jazz?" many of your students hear something that they believe speaks directly to them.

It's been years since California teacher Alan Sitomer added a little bumpin' flava to his language arts lessons at Lynwood High School, transforming his classroom and his students, too. Beginning with a single bridge that he built between Welsh poet Dylan Thomas (he of "Do not go gentle into that good night") and murdered rapper Tupac Shakur ("The question is, will I live?") Sitomer began finding ways to bring "fresh relevance to timeless themes."

"I got started using hip-hop in the classroom because my students were spectacularly disengaged from the classic curriculum. They roll out all these materials when you become a new teacher—do this, do that—but the kids don't see their lives reflected in those materials.

"I decided to meet them where they live."

There is one thing you can do as a teacher, that's more important than anything else, to help them and help you, suggests Sarah Montgomery-Glinski, co-director of the educational initiative at the New York-based Hip-Hop Association and a high school special education teacher herself. And it's this:

"Connect with your students. Don't be afraid."

For him, the lyrics—scrubbed of all profanity, misogyny, homophobia, or other offense—offer a valid source of imagery, alliteration, personification, or other literary devices.

Gettin' JIGGY Wit' It

Where they once stared blankly and scored near the bottom of standardized tests, Sitomer's students now are energized learners, strong academic performers, and proof that it's possible to use hip-hop as a tool for engagement and resource for lesson planning. And, as for Sitomer, a former California State Teacher of the Year, his methods have become so sought-after that he's become a book author and coveted speaker.

"When I started this, I was vilified. 'That's not real teaching!'" Sitomer recalls. "But when you look at my scores, I have some of the highest California exit-exam scores in the state. [Ninety-eight percent of his kids passed, compared with 57 percent of Lynwood's overall.] I attribute that to the fact that my students are engaged in learning. . . . Once the students are engaged, you can go anywhere."

Your colleagues who use hip-hop in the classroom almost all consider it a tool to get somewhere else. This isn't Hip-Hop 101. "I'm teaching artistry, not the artist," Sitomer says.

For him, the lyrics—scrubbed of all profanity, misogyny, homophobia, or other offense—offer a valid source of imagery, alliteration, personification, or other literary devices. Often he'll pair a hip-hop artist with a classic poet to teach a specific standard. Sometimes, because the 40-something doesn't even pretend to know what kids are listening to, he'll assign his students, who are mostly Black or Hispanic, the task of finding answers in their own digital collections.

For Adam Recktenwald, an art teacher who teaches a multidisciplinary humanities course at suburban East Brunswick High School in New Jersey, even the questionable language offers opportunities. During a unit on diversity, discussions about stereotypical language, the way that we communicate with each other, whether positively or negatively, can be stimulated by hip-hop. "What exactly is he talking about? Why are you listening to that? Do you really understand what he's saying?"

(You might not have any idea what he's really saying either. Recktenwald advises taking a look at www.urbandictionary.com, a sometimes unreliable, often shocking guide to the way kids talk.)

Modern culture connects with kids, he's found. Clips of race comics, like Dave Chappelle or Russell Peters, bring home more lessons about censorship and societal values. "A lot of our students feel our society is post-racist. Like, 'We're so not-racist it's OK to be racist again. . . .'

"We give them an opportunity to talk about things that they wouldn't otherwise—and these are things they should talk about before they go away to college and enter a larger group that's even more diverse," Recktenwald says. "There are definitely students that have wake-up calls . . . that are learning to make connections."

Bring the Noise

A quick history lesson: Hip-hop first appeared in New York City in the 1970s, mostly in Black communities. At first, it was mostly unrecorded and focused on danceable percussive beats and narrative raps.

In the 1980s, the music grew more complicated. With new technology, artists commonly "sampled" other songs and laid down multi-layered beats with raps that were becoming more metaphorical and socially conscious. At the same time, artists like LL Cool J and Public Enemy, who released the political entreaty, "Fight the Power," in 1989, started to make it big. ("Our freedom of speech is freedom or death. We got to fight the powers that be!")

"These are artists who are making statements. If you go back and listen to that music, it's poetic," Recktenwald says. Since then, with the rise of "gangsta rap" and commercial rewards for the most offensive artists, it's tough to find the good stuff, Recktenwald acknowledges. "A lot of people think hip-hop equals pornography. But probably what they've heard is the least talented, least poetic. What's accessible is garbage."

Of course, to many educators, it's all garbage—you'd rather spend time with Ludacris than Steinbeck? "I teach literature and kids really respond to dinosaur stuff like *Of Mice and Men*, and *Frankenstein*. Of course they can only respond if they're exposed to them," says one English teacher. "It's our job as educators to expose them to decent ideas—and combat crass culture."

With new technology, artists commonly "sampled" other songs and laid down multi-layered beats with raps that were becoming more metaphorical and socially conscious.

"Students need to learn about literature," adds another. "We're doing them a huge disservice when we manipulate the curriculum just to make a connection."

Still, if you want the motivating beat of hip-hop without its baggage, you may ignore commercial artists altogether. In recent years, the buzz around hip-hop educational products has reached a new crescendo.

One of the first was Brooklyn-based Flocabulary ("Rocking harder than your grandma's chair," www.flocabulary.com), which started off with SAT words and definitions set to catchy raps but has since branched out to U.S. history, science, and math curricula. More recently, Black Gold Edutainment, www.hiphop-edu.com, wowed audiences at the 2008 NEA Representative Assembly.

Or take a look at some of your colleagues, like Detroit-area middle school teacher D.J. Duey, www.mrduey.com. "Solid! People at the party are getting real crowded. So close together they can't move around!" rhymes Duey in his physical science rap, "State of Matter." Or, check out two New York City educators who have teamed up to teach reading and math at www.sing2school.com.

"Kids know every rap song, right? But then they can't remember the definition of obsequiousness," says Alex Rappaport, a former tutor and Flocabulary founder. He points to memory research that shows the brain is wired in a way that makes music helpful for memory recall. (There's a reason you remember all the lyrics to "Summer of '69"!) Plus, the kids just dig it. "We've been in a lot of urban schools, especially in New York and California, and the response is: 'This is something I'm interested in. I get it.'"

Rappaport is a recent college graduate and both East Coast hipsters, Recktenwald and Montgomery-Glinski, also are in their 20s. But none of them believe that hip-hop is a teaching tool for the youngest workers only.

"There's room for anybody to use just about any form of art in the classroom. I don't feel ashamed to talk about Greek and Roman sculpture. I don't feel silly talking about Frank Simusic that has confused and bemused me for years. When I wrote a book explaining why, a common response (to the extent that there were any!) was that the whole idea that anybody thinks hiphop is more than just good music was a figment of my imagination.

But bookshelves groan with work describing rap as "prophetic" and breathlessly exploring the possibility of a "hip hop revolution" and its potential to "motivate" young people. This *Atlantic* roundtable is cut from that cloth. Whence this idea that music, rather than effort, can change things politically?

For example, the participants look back fondly on the days when more of the music was "political," with Alyssa Rosenberg opining that it's unrealistic to decree that musicians follow our bidding and be "constructive." But this whole wing of the discussion presupposes a hypothetical possibility that hiphop could serve some kind of purpose beyond being just entertainment, that it is at least worth discussion whether rappers have some kind of "responsibility." Gautham Nagesh even thinks that way back, rap actually did play a crucial part in making people aware of ghetto life ("rap has played a key role in raising awareness of issues such as urban poverty").

Hip Hop Is Only Entertainment

The question here is: what is the purpose of this supposedly politically important rap supposed to be? Let's even say consciousness is raised: now that Scarsdale Chad [Scarsdale is an wealthy, white suburb of New York City] knows what it's like growing up in the 'hood, then what? What does Chad do besides walk down the street lurching and mouthing along to Tupac or whoever it was he learned this from in the early nineties? The consciousness was raised—and what legislation did it create? In a history book 100 years from now, we will see it written that "Because of hiphop raising consciousness of ghetto poverty starting in the late 1980s, _____." Fill in the blank. Note the difficulty.

My sense is that my even bringing up this issue of purpose is seen as somehow beside the point, but that very impatience, the grouchy feeling that my asking this means that there is something I don't "get," is revealing of a serious problem with what we have been taught to think of as politics. Namely, we assume that it is meaningfully political to strike poses and say things rather than do things.

Few are aware of it, but this traces back to the way smart people have for decades been misinterpeting Antonio Gramsci, the Italian political theorist. The key text would seem to be *The Prison Notebooks*, where he argued that the ruling class creates ideological structures, such as educational systems, that support their interests while obscuring the evil underpinnings of society. Subordinate ("subaltern") groups accept these ideas and end up oppressing themselves. Thus they must counteract the "hegemony" through attempts to revise cultural conceptions.

Rap that was about [political] solutions . . . would be about as plausible as opera about physical fitness.

So, under this analysis, which starts with intellectuals and spreads outward to the general consciousness, rappers are presenting a new Cultural Paradigm, with their academic celebrants as conduits of that new "message" to the ruling class. Poor blacks are the subalterns; Washington, DC, [former secretary of education] William Bennett, and suburban whites who don't "see" blacks and preserve their "white privilege" are the Hegemony, and so on.

But Gramsci himself would be surprised to see how his ideas have been recruited for the subtle and complex race situation in America of the late twentieth century. He was a practicing Communist who wrote *The Prison Notebooks* from, well, prison, where he spent the last ten years of his life. He wrote in reference to working-class and peasant folk for whom the barriers to advancement were concrete and required no careful indoctrination to understand in the way that the black victim orthodoxy does today.

And the problem is that in black America and beyond, as historian David Steigerwald puts it, "the more the intellectuals have analyzed cultural hegemony, the less real political effect their radicalism has had." He notes that "Where the hard and gradual work of organizing revolution is dreamed away and the Left becomes willingly content with 'cultural resistance,' the best radicals can hope for is directionless, feeble, and scattered opposition to the state of things."

Gramsci did not mean that striking anti-authoritarian poses on pop recordings, videos, and posters was meaningful sociopolitical activity. This is how modern academics have distorted his argumentation, and is the source of the idea that hiphop's "subalterns" have accomplished something sublime because their lyrics disrespect authority.

What these roundtable participants don't seem to quite understand is that this is all even political rap could ever do. It is the DNA of the form to be confrontational—whether about politics, women, social pecking order (i.e. the in-your-face bling, etc.) or anything else. Rap that was about solutions, as Rosenberg calls for, would be about as plausible as opera about physical fitness.

Lyrics That Offer No Solutions

Take Cam'ron's "I Hate My Job," which I have commended for even broaching the very real problem of getting a job as an ex-con. There are solutions a-plenty, as I have also blogged here about: but how many of us can really imagine a rap about getting an apartment, waiting for a driver's license, or *holding down* a job? It's a meaningless issue. As Nagesh notes, when rappers have tried to just sit back and celebrate that Obama is in—i.e. nothing to be mad about—they don't quite know what to do.

I really like the new idea floating around that hiphop may have helped elect Barack Obama. Once more, that impulse to see hiphop as something other than fun. If one must speak of hiphop and Obama in the same breath—beyond noting that he, rather unsurprisingly of a black man under 50, listens to some—then what Obama has shown us is what a real revolution is, as opposed to the kind written about with 20-dollar words in books.

The idea that hiphop, because it makes the body feel good to move to it and it makes the soul feel good to hear out angry young black men, can be transmuted into changing the world is . . . nonsensical.

To wit: after decades of people wondering when the Great Hiphop Revolution might be coming—tell me no one was waiting for that since Public Enemy and explain stuff like Vote or Die and Russell Simmons' Hip-Hop Summit Action Network well into this current decade—Obama strode in and galvanized exactly the demographic in question with real political organizing, with inspiration that was about something other than having your middle finger stuck up, with, in a word, work.

It is unclear to me that hiphop played a significant part in making Obama president. Certainly it brought some people to some concerts where people registered to vote, but that very thing made no difference in the 2004 election and I am unaware of evidence that it tipped the scales to Obama this time. A thought experiment: if hiphop didn't exist and Obama had come along anyway, I see no reason to suppose that Obama would not now be President.

Nagesh seems to think that hiphop moguls like Jay-Z helped get white people used to the idea of black authority figures—but that revolution in thought started long before. There has been a general "browning" of our culture that has accustomed all of us to blackness as mainstream that Leon Wynter, in a book that never got enough attention partly because it was published around the first anniversary of 9/11, dates to 1980, in the commercial where Mean Joe Greene tossed an admiring white boy his jersey.

Politics is work. Hiphop is music. Hua Hsu seems to get this, although it's less that it's "unfair" to expect rap to be "constructive"—implying that it could be—than that it is purely illogical. The idea that hiphop, because it makes the body feel good to move to it and it makes the soul feel good to hear out angry young black men, can be transmuted into changing the world is narcotic but nonsensical. Wherever hiphop is ever "going," we can be sure it will not be in a constructive direction, anymore than fashions in the color of cars. And it shouldn't "concern" us in the least.

Society Will Not Suffer If Music Lyrics Are Censored

Malcolm X Abram

Malcolm X Abram is the music writer for the Akron (OH) Beacon Journal.

Television and radio talk show host Don Imus's racist and degrading comments about members of the Rutgers University women's basketball team (most of whom are black) resulted in MSNBC firing him from his job at the network. Whether Imus should have been fired is almost beside the point; his departure will not change society's attitude toward black women. The misogyny spewed by rappers will continue until the public decides it is no longer going to pay for this music. Then, and only then, will the record companies take notice. Rap music today has no substantive effect on society. Attitudes toward black women, as well as attitudes toward guns, money, and violence, will only change when adults talk to their children about making different choices in the music they listen to.

I couldn't care less about the adventures of Don Imus, but if it helps remove the carcass of Anna Nicole Smith and her strange, sad life and sadder death out of the news, then let's discuss it, shall we?

The comments made by Don Imus disparaging the predominantly black Rutgers women's basketball team are not analogous to the misogynistic lyrics found in many rappers' songs.

Jean Grae (or any female rapper whose genitals aren't her primary marketing tool) with the same resources they happily commit to the unimaginative, pandering lunkheads of the G-Unit (especially that child-slapping, crap-rhyming idiot Tony Yayo), that would be useful.

Of course, even if mainstream rappers were to collectively develop a social conscience next week, it couldn't save the 'hood any more than 1960s protest rock and folk songs stopped the Vietnam War. But certainly a genre made by us and (originally) for us dependent on words should illustrate the joy and pain of life, love and even hate, and make us dance without hindering the emotional growth, self-image and healthy gender interaction of its listeners.

The Public Must Demand Change

The Al Sharptons and Jesse Jacksons can raise their voices in protest all they want, as they and others have done for years but nothing will change until the buying public demands it and one reason popular rap seems so creatively stunted is that guns, cars, hos and the acquisition of overpriced products still sells.

As for hip-hop's Golden Era (roughly, 1986 to 1995), often lionized by many of us older hip-hop fans, there was still misogyny and violence to be found in the music, but there was also Public Enemy and Boogie Down Productions, commanding you to be proud of your blackness and your nappy hair, and to look beyond the block to question authority. There was De La Soul and A Tribe Called Quest and Pete Rock and C.L. Smooth, enjoying the art of rhyming and crate-digging for beats, and there was Queen Latifah being strong and encouraging young women to ask "who you callin' a b----!?"

Many of rap's young fans are raised in similar conditions to their heroes, and often have little parental or other tangible guidance to help them separate their favorite rapper's tough guy cliches from how grown men and women should actually conduct themselves and treat one another, in a society that's not interested in their survival.

As for the suburban kids who are still getting their vicarious thrills from the music, they don't care if the 'hood they're so fascinated with burns down tomorrow, because the whole culture is just a cool, aural blaxploitation flick to them. And once they get bored, with one quick trip to Hot Topic they can put on tight pants, stare at their navels and become emo kids, punks, goths or whatever the cool kids at school are doing.

Any real exchange of ideas about . . . why guns, easy women, products and money are the quick track to the Billboard charts, or why that combination is the American Dream to many rappers/fans from poor communities . . . should happen because it's important for parents, guardians, older relatives and authority figures to talk to their children about the music they listen to.

Parents Must Guide Their Children

If the aforementioned execs and the rappers who work for them all saw their bottom lines drop precipitously (sales of rap CDs did fall significantly in 2006, but the whole industry is down), then suddenly the focus of "blazing hip-hop" would shift to rhymes about the state of the union, the relative cuteness of kittens versus puppies, or whatever subject might recapture the listening public's attention and wallets.

Please, let me be clear. Any real exchange of ideas about "the state of hip-hop" or why guns, easy women, products and money are the quick track to the Billboard charts, or why that combination is the American Dream to many rappers/fans from poor communities, cannot happen because some old guy got fired for being the same insensitive jerk he was way before Melle Mel said he was "close to the edge."

The conversation has to happen because everyone should want daughters, sisters and around-the-way girls, as well as sons, brothers and homeboys, to grow up respecting themselves and each other. It should happen because it's important for parents, guardians, older relatives and authority figures to talk to their children about the music they listen to and the shows they watch. And because you cannot rely on musicians or record companies to put the mental and emotional needs of the community, even their own, before the financial needs of their hungry bank accounts.

Society Suffers from Any Form of Censorship

Julie Polter

Julie Polter is an associate editor at Sojourners Magazine.

Given its ability to inspire and unite people, music can be a threat to governments and religious groups. In many countries, musicians have been tortured and killed in an effort to silence their words. Because music has a unique ability to comfort, console, and heal, any attempt by a government or religious group to control society's access to music decreases the quality of each individual's life. Once a song has been banned because it is perceived as dangerous to society, it is only a matter of time before all forms of expression that the ruling authority disapproves of are forbidden.

To sing or to die: now I will begin. There's no force that can silence me.—Pablo Neruda, "Epic Song"

In a world so torn by poverty and war, perhaps music can seem like a secondary concern. But as Christians know so well, music feeds the spirit, comforts the downtrodden, strengthens the weary, and can give words a power they do not possess on paper. Imagine life without your favorite hymn or the song that safely channeled your teenage rebellion, or the anthem of peace or protest that still stirs you. Imagine life without Bach or Handel, or Neil Young, or Billie Holiday singing "Strange Fruit" (dismissed in its day by *Time* magazine as "a prime piece of musical propaganda").

Julie Polter, "Replacing Songs with Silence," *Sojourners Magazine*, vol. 34, November 2005. Copyright © 2005 by *Sojourners*. All rights reserved. Reprinted with permission from *Sojourners*, (800) 714-7474, www.sojo.net.

Imagine if someone literally took away your song. Wouldn't you hunger for it like bread?

Life Without Music Is Diminished

When a government or powerful religious or ethnic group tries to turn off the music, the stakes are high. Music is another way to hear the news and a means to find common passion between very different peoples. In this way silence, or a restricted diet of state-approved tunes, can diminish us. But the more immediate and sometimes tragic cost is borne by the artists around the globe who have faced intimidation, loss of livelihood, imprisonment, torture, and even death for recording, performing, or distributing their music:

- South Africa revoked singer Miriam Makeba's citizenship and right of return after her 1963 testimony about apartheid before the United Nations.

- Populist Chilean folk/political singer and songwriter Victor Jara was one of several musicians who supported the successful 1970 campaign of Salvador Allende to become president of Chile. When a 1973 military coup overturned the Allende government, Jara was among the thousands of citizens subsequently tortured and executed. His torturers reportedly broke his hands so that he couldn't play his guitar; his final lyrics, written on scraps of paper during the few days before he was killed, were smuggled out by survivors.

- Argentinean concert pianist Miguel Angel Estrella was committed to promoting music education among the poorest people in his country; this work was considered subversive by the military government that came into power in Argentina in 1976. In 1977, Estrella, temporarily living and working in Uruguay, was arrested by armed representatives of the Uruguayan government (which was sympathetic to Argentina's rulers). He was tortured, repeatedly brought before military tribunals, and imprisoned for more than two years before he was released. According to a statement Estrella gave to the anti-censorship organization Freemuse, his torturers would say, "We know that you are not a member of the guerrilla, but you are worse, because with your piano, your 'charisma,' you can put the 'negrada' working class into your pocket."

Music's Power Threatens Tyrants

Why do tyrants fear the singer? Why do those who would control institutions and culture fear artistic expression often as much as they fear a free press? Because music has power to influence emotions, thoughts, and behavior. Anabaptists fleeing severe persecution in the 1500s wrote and sang a prodigious number of hymns—despite the fact that to be heard might result in death—celebrating their faith and preparing them for the possibility of martyrdom. U.S. civil rights protesters and South African freedom fighters used singing as a vehicle of unity, courage, and defiance as they faced down dogs, guns, and mobs. And, lest we forget that any power can be used for good or evil, Rwandan radio broadcast songs encouraging the killing of Hutus by Tutsis before and during the 1994 massacres.

On the other hand, music is not a magic remote control, capable of changing hearts and minds with a single note, a single song, or even an entire symphony. A musician may influence those who listen, but no musician or songwriter is capable of single-handedly turning our sons into skinheads, our daughters into anarchists, or ourselves into saints or sinners.

Jonathan Trew, writing in the Nov. 14, 2004, edition of the *Scotland on Sunday* newspaper, captures the ambiguity inherent in understanding the power of music: " . . . to suggest music does not influence actions is nonsense. It is a question of degree. The most sickening lyrics will not make the man in the displeasure of fundamentalists with both the music presented and her mere presence as a woman on TV. In July her male co-host fled to Sweden to escape harassment and death threats.

Which are more dangerous—songs or those who would silence them?

Musicians can be treated as tools of political maneuvering. In Nigeria, Afrobeat star Femi Kuti—son of the late legendary musician and political activist Fela Kuti—has had one song banned for years for racy content, while raunchy Western songs continue to receive airplay. Kuti contends that it is a back-door means for the government to disrupt his work, which often features political songs with commentary on government corruption. During the run-up to last March's parliamentary elections in Zimbabwe, several popular musicians were recruited to write songs supporting President Robert Mugabe's campaign; they subsequently suffered a nosedive in their careers as fans refused to buy their records or attend their concerts. But if they had declined Mugabe's request, their music likely would have been banned from radio, which is state-owned. In Belarus, the government of dictator Aleksandr Lukashenko banned from radio the music of several of the country's top bands after they performed at a concert protesting Lukashenko's rule.

The common thread in all these situations is the desire by an institution or group to control and suppress free expression. Those fortunate enough to live in a relatively stable democracy have the option of debate—sometimes messy but rarely dangerous—over whether artistic content is somehow beyond the pale. But when debate is dangerous, or when even one's faith or language is considered a threat, the key question is put into high relief: Which are more dangerous—songs or those who would silence them?

Hip-Hop Lyrics Reflect the Reality of Black Urban Culture

Nick Marino

Nick Marino is managing editor of Paste *magazine. He also has written for the* Boston Globe, Entertainment Weekly, *and* Spin.

Blues music is often described as a dying genre; however, the similarities between blues and hip-hop may indicate that hip-hop and rap are the newest reembodiment of the blues. While hip-hop is often criticized for being overly focused on violence and sex, the case can be made that it, as well as rap, reflect black culture—just as the blues always has. Where blues singers, such as Muddy Waters, sang about the lives of African Americans in the South, today's rappers and hip-hop singers describe the life of African Americans in urban neighborhoods. The common denominators are anger and pain.

Mississippi Hill Country pioneer R.L. Burnside, soul-blues vocalist Little Milton and the explosive singer-guitarist Paul "Wine" Jones all passed away in 2005, intensifying the nagging sense that blues music is dying off.

But the blues aren't dying. They're just being reincarnated—in the form of hip-hop. In the last 25 years, as traditional voice-and-guitar blues have waned, rap has come to embody virtually everything that has made the genre matter. Like the blues, rap is the black popular music of its time. It focuses attention on some of the country's most depressed corners. It courses with the kind of visceral anger and pain that made the blues necessary in the first place.

Blues and Hip-Hop Reflect Life

Even though "it's not the same type of music or don't sound the same," says Mississippi-raised rapper David Banner, "basically we all saying the same thing: We hurtin'. You know, we hurtin'. And that's the blues."

Slaves used rhythmic proto-blues work songs to make forced labor tolerable; today Atlanta rapper Young Jeezy provides fat beats and "Thug Motivation" for hustlers working drug-infested streets. In the heart of the 20th century, Son House and Muddy Waters helped define African-American life in the Mississippi Delta; today the Game and 50 Cent paint pictures of life in Compton, Calif., and southside Jamaica, Queens.

Slaves used rhythmic proto-blues work songs to make forced labor tolerable; today Atlanta rapper Young Jeezy provides fat beats and "Thug Motivation" for hustlers working drug-infested streets.

Musical improvisation has become lyrical freestyling. Instrumental prowess has become verbal virtuosity. Robert Johnson's "Hellhound on My Trail" has become Biggie Smalls' "Warning." The guitar has become the turntable.

"As original American musics," Public Enemy leader Chuck D wrote in 2003, "both blues and rap are laced with attitude and coded double-entendre. One can easily find comparisons in the lives of both Tupac Shakur and Little Walter; a turntablist like DJ Babu of the Dilated Peoples and the behind-the-head playing style of Texas great T-Bone Walker; the throaty rawness of DMX and Howlin' Wolf—even in the way record companies then and now hustle the sounds from 'the hood' back to the hood, and even abroad. . . . The similarities are baffling."

Similarities are most obvious in the Memphis area, thanks to film director Craig Brewer and musician Cody Dickinson of the North Mississippi Allstars.

Brewer's "Hustle & Flow" paints a sympathetic portrait of a drug-dealing Memphis pimp trying to express his frustrations through rap lyrics. The director's next movie, "Black Snake Moan," will star Samuel L. Jackson as a former bluesman returning to the music.

"I gotta be honest," Brewer says. "I don't think many of the modern guys were listening to the old-school guys. I don't know if Dre, when he was a kid, was listening to Howlin' Wolf and Son House. But I don't think Son House and Charley Patton were necessarily listening to the drum rhythms and the shouts and hollers from Jamaica and Africa, either.

"But I do think that there is something to be said for having limited resources and limited tools and using them. So you look at a man and a drum, you look at a man with one guitar, and you look at a man with one beat machine—and the rest is up to that combination. The magic comes from the right man with that right one single instrument and the voice that he allows you to witness and to experience."

Just across the Mississippi state line, the Allstars are fusing rap and roots music into a kaleidoscopic post-blues sound. In September [2005], they released an album that, in addition to psychedelic guitars and floorboard-stomping beats, incorporated chanted vocals from Memphis rapper Al Kapone.

Neither the Blues nor Rap Glorify Poverty

This month [December 2005], the Allstars released the six-song "Chopped and Screwed EP," which applies a slow and swervy production style associated with Houston rap to the band's bluesy groove. Allstars drummer Cody Dickinson also has founded the online record label Diamond D, which provides an outlet for regional rappers. Dickinson calls Southern hip-hop artists "inspiring."

"It's fresh, and they've got good ideas," he says. "And the fact that maybe their parents would dance dirty in a juke joint with a dirt floor and they don't want to do that anymore; they want to have polished shoes with a gold necklace around their neck—frankly, I don't blame them."

That's a point blues scholar Elijah Wald suggested in last year's "Escaping the Delta," a book-length corrective to much of the mythology that contemporary fans, often older white listeners, place on the black blues. "Black fans," Wald wrote, "have never been charmed by poverty, or needed a sordid atmosphere in order to feel that they were having a real blues experience. While white fans drink straight whiskey to get into a blues mood, Muddy Waters drank only champagne, and insisted that it be the real French stuff."

In this context, the blues lament "Broke and Ain't Got a Dime" is no more a celebration of poverty than 50 Cent's "In My Hood" is a glorification of life in the slums. Young white rap fans may join older white blues fans in romanticizing urban housing projects and backwoods juke joints, but, according to Wald's book, "The most popular and influential blues players were rarely stuck playing the lousiest joints. Waters and Johnson were known for their clean, sharp suits, and they played for the hippest crowds their neighborhoods provided."

Rap and Hip-Hop Will Evolve

Likewise, 50 drapes himself in platinum and diamonds. He left Queens, N.Y., and lives in Mike Tyson's old Connecticut mansion, fulfilling a meteoric American Dream that the prewar bluesmen could hardly have imagined. And he's done it all using a familiar formula. He may be more explicit than a bluesman like Robert Johnson, but 50's subject matter—sex and violence, as evidenced by his hit "P.I.M.P."—remains largely the same. After all, it was Johnson who, almost 70 years ago, sang "I'm gonna beat my woman until I'm satisfied."

In conversation, Wald stresses that the rap-blues parallel works best if you compare contemporary rap not with contemporary blues but with the blues of the early 20th century.

"I just don't see rap surviving in the way blues has survived," he says. "That isn't necessarily a bad thing. I mean, keep in mind how blues has survived. It has survived largely in the white community as a barroom music, for better or worse."

Wald finds it hard to imagine an aging Snoop Dogg performing in the Sheraton lounge for 60-year-old fans in their good clothes, the way blues fans might today. He asks, "In 20 years will the white kids who are now buying Snoop Dogg be interested in going to a club to see white kids do Snoop Dogg covers? I doubt it."

Since its inception more than a quarter-century ago, hip-hop has been dismissed as a fad. For the music's many fans, this has been a particularly bothersome insult. But given the life-support on which the blues have survived, perhaps hip-hop purists should hope rap runs its course and then vanishes—making way for the next incarnation. After all, pain and anger never die; they just inhabit new souls.

Hip-Hop Lyrics Do Not Reflect the Reality of Most African Americans

John McWhorter

John McWhorter is a contributing editor at the New Republic, *a senior fellow at the Manhattan Institute, and a lecturer at Columbia University. His books include* The Power of Babel: A Natural History of Language *and* Doing Our Own Thing: The Degradation of Language and Music in America and Why We Should, Like, Care.

The argument that hip-hop and rap accurately reflect the problems of black Americans is, at best, a weak one. It's an oxymoron to talk about "conscious" rappers and their messages. Many African Americans have been able to achieve the "American Dream" without resorting to the violence espoused in many hip-hop and rap songs. Simply put, the lyrics are not really relevant to most African Americans' lives. The lyrics can be catchy and have rhythms to which you can dance, but they offer nothing in the way of setting out or trying to seek solutions to the very real problems that many urban blacks face. There's more to life than violence, sex, and alcohol.

Word on the street is that hip-hop is a message, the black CNN. Anyone who questions that winds up at the bottom of a verbal dog pile. Such traitors, we're told, just don't listen to enough of the music—that, in particular, the work of "conscious" rappers would change their minds.

Please. One can take a good dose of Talib Kweli, Common, Mos Def and Kanye "Bush doesn't care about black people" West and still see nothing that resembles any kind of "message" that people truly committed to forging change would recognize. Hip-hop, "conscious" or not, is music, and that's it.

For one thing, a lot of the "conscious" work sounds as much like street fighting as the gangsta stuff—an upturned middle finger set to a beat. Yes, Mos Def and Talib Kweli decorate their raps with calls to stop smoking and drinking, starry-eyed timeouts when they sing the praises of their baby daughters and vague calls for black Americans to look sharp.

But there's a decent amount of that even in so-called gangsta rap, such as Tupac Shakur's chronicle of the vicious cycle of urban poverty in "Papa'z Song," or artist Nas' hope that he will be able to redeem his past through his child in "The World Is Yours."

But why so violent? Why, exactly, must "consciousness" so often sound like a street fight?

Meanwhile, Kweli tells us that when he's at the mike "you get hit like a deer standin' still in the light" and how in one competition he "smacked them in they face with a metaphor."

OK, he means it in the abstract. But why so violent? Why, exactly, must "consciousness" so often sound like a street fight? The "conscious" rappers just relocate 50 Cent's cops-and-robbers battle from the street to the slam contest.

No Real Substance to Hip-Hop Lyrics

I know: "Politics" means questioning authority. But street battle is not the only metaphor for civil rights activism. Since the Sixties, millions of black people have achieved middle-class or even affluent status, founded businesses and attained higher degrees in this country, and very few of them did so by smacking somebody, literally or in the abstract.

It's true that violence is a matter of atmosphere in the "conscious" work. But I have a hard time gleaning exactly what the "message" is beyond, roughly, "wake up"—which does not qualify as constructive counsel in times as complex as ours.

Take Kweli again, in "The Proud." The "message": Blacks are worn down by oppression, the cops are corrupt thugs who either killed Tupac or know who did, and "we survive." But how we get beyond that is, apparently, beside the point.

Mos Def's "Mr. N----" first shows us the improper black thug we all could do without, but then argues that whites see all blacks the same way many blacks see the thug. It's a great piece in the formal sense.

It sounds good set to a narcotic beat full of exciting cut-ins, but it offers nothing to the struggling black woman with children trying to make the best of things after her welfare time limit runs out.

But how many people's "consciousnesses" in our moment are unaware that racist bias still exists? How does saying it for the nth time teach anyone how to make the best of themselves despite reality's imperfections?

Or Kanye West's famous "Jesus Walks" cut is less "inspirational" than catchy. It's about Jesus; that's nice. But one more announcement that black America is in a "war" against racism inspires, well, nothing, nor do other bonbons West gives us on "College Dropout," such as the notion that crack makes white men rich or that blacks are only placed in high positions as window dressing.

Maybe these "conscious" lyrics are better than gangsta raps about tying women to beds and shooting them dead. But the politics are a typical brand of self-perpetuating, unfocused leftism. It sounds good set to a narcotic beat full of exciting cut-ins, but it offers nothing to the struggling black woman with children trying to make the best of things after her welfare time limit runs out.

Lyrics Should Offer Solutions to Problems

Yes, her. In 1991, Tupac's "Brenda's Got a Baby" told about a single mom who tries to throw her daughter in the trash, turns to prostitution and is murdered. Many Brendas at that time went on welfare only to find that in 1996 it was limited to a five-year cap. So, these days, "Brenda's Just Off Welfare" and is one of the working poor. How about "consciously" rapping—a lot—about the difficulties Brenda faces today?

We do not look to raps for detailed procedural prescriptives, like government reports on how to improve school test scores. But there are places raps could easily go, still blazing with poetic fireworks.

Why do "conscious" rappers have so little interest in the political issues that directly affect poor black people's lives?

What about the black men coming out of jail and trying to find their way after long sentences in the wake of the crack culture 15 years ago? There would be a "message" beyond the usual one simply deploring that the men are in jail in the first place.

Why do "conscious" rappers have so little interest in the political issues that directly affect poor black people's lives? Could it be because those issues do not usually lend themselves to calls for smacking people and making the streets run red? If so, then chalk up one more for people who do not see hip-hop as politically constructive.

Rappers Confuse Attitude with Activism

The "conscious" rappers themselves make the "message" analysis even harder to fall for because they tend to squirm under the label. "They keep trying to slip the 'conscious rapper' thing on me," Mos Def says. "They try to get me because I'm supposed to be more articulate, I'm supposed to be not like the other Negroes, to get me to say something against my brothers. I'm not going out like that, man."

So it would be "going out" even to question the theatrical savagery that hip-hop's critics fail to see the good in?

"Conscious" rap, like gangsta rap, is ultimately all about spitting in the eye of the powers that be. But this is precisely what the millions of blacks making the best of themselves in modern America have not done. And contrary to what we are often led to believe, spitting is not serious activism. It's merely attitude.

There is not a thing wrong with "conscious rap" fans enjoying the beats and the rhymes and even valuing the sprinkles of an awareness of something beyond guns, Hennessy and women's behinds. But if we have gotten to the point that we are treating even this "conscious" work as serious civil rights activism, then black America is in even worse trouble than we thought.

Hip-Hop Lyrics Are No More Degrading to Women Than Other Media

Nida Khan

Nida Khan is a news correspondent with WRKS 98.7 FM in New York. She also is an independent print and radio producer and journalist who works on the production of Keepin It Real, *the Reverend Al Sharpton's nationally syndicated radio show.*

It's unfair to single out hip-hop and rap as the only sources of sexism and misogyny. Their roots can be found in society as a whole. Women of color are also underrepresented and too often portrayed in purely sexual terms in Hollywood, but this does not garner as much attention as do the images of women in hip-hop and rap. Rappers and hip-hop musicians have profound ideas to express. Some, such as Jay-Z and 50 Cent, have become great successes. Most, however, are held hostage by record companies that control the types of music these artists can release and who are, ultimately, only interested in making as much money as they can off the backs of these artists.

"Hip-hop is the CNN of the ghetto"—words spoken by legendary artist Chuck D of Public Enemy years before Puffy became a household name and bling a term used by actual CNN anchors. Serving as a mirror to such societal ills as poverty, injustice, drugs and violence, hip-hop—or more specifically rap music—has brought realities of urban life and mainstream systematic privilege to the forefront of discussion.

MCs, aka rappers, have opened wounds that many would prefer remained covered via methods that both educate and entertain. Now this mechanism for empowerment and communication is under attack yet again.

While Don Imus searched for a defense against his use of the now notorious words "nappy headed hos" in reference to the Rutgers women's basketball team, he was successful in scapegoating the often-targeted genre of hip-hop. But what Imus and the average citizen fail to grasp is the foundation of this culture or the notion that what you hear on radio airwaves and see on TV doesn't encompass the plethora of diversity within the music.

Serving as a mirror to such societal ills as poverty, injustice, drugs and violence, hip-hop—or more specifically rap music—has brought realities of urban life and mainstream systematic privilege to the forefront of discussion.

Misogyny Is a Problem Throughout Society

For several years I've worked within the hip-hop industry in a multitude of capacities. From my vantage point at record labels, recording studios and finally as a music journalist, I've had the honor of sitting down and picking the brains of many hip-hop poets. And *poetry* and *expression* is exactly what they produce: words and ideas conjured over the hottest beats. Rappers take complex ideas and transform them into catchy lyrics and rhyming sequences with astuteness and intense precision. Imagine the endless boundaries of MCs if they were all given equal access to education and opportunity that we espouse but rarely see in this country. A chance to pursue the American Dream is precisely what rappers under attack have worked to achieve.

Take a look at the 50 Cents and Jay-Zs of the world. Self-made millionaires, they battled extreme circumstances and in the process established companies that employ and empower others shut out of corporate America. In response to the on-going controversy, several people have stepped forward. "We are proactive, not just reactive to the Don Imus so-called backlash," explains Dr. Ben Chavis, president/CEO of Russell Simmons's Hip-Hop Summit Action Network, after he and Simmons made recommendations for the recording industry to bleep the words ho, bitch and n----- on the airwaves and on clean CDs.

"The truth is misogyny is not a hip-hop created problem. Misogyny is a deep-seated American society problem that is embedded in the historical evolution of the United States as a nation." The recommendations are meant, he says, to forestall governmental intrusion "on the rights of artists in a demo-cratic society. This is important, and there are some in the media that just don't get it. Self regulation by the industry is not censorship. Good corporate social responsibility is not censorship."

Why don't we go after the millionaire and billionaire movie directors/producers of the world who represent minority women a majority of the time as the exotic other or the overly sexualized temptress, and minority men as criminals?

The shift in dynamic from Imus to hip-hop utterly amazes me. Granted I don't condone use of words like ho and bitch towards myself or any other woman, but I understand along with Dr. Ben that rap music isn't the only forum where we see this.

Why don't we target the representation of women and people of color in Hollywood? Why don't we go after the mil-lionaire and billionaire movie directors/producers of the world who represent minority women a majority of the time as the exotic other or the overly sexualized temptress, and minority men as criminals?

Blacks Are Exploited More by Whites

Before blaming everything on one facet, we need to analyze all of pop culture and media representation at large. MCs may have an audience via their music, but until you see a Snoop Dogg or a Ludacris with his own televised programming in mainstream news you simply can't juxtapose Imus and hip-hop.

Until rappers have the kind of major network platform that Imus had and will have again, they are not fair game for attack. On the contrary, we need to explore and criticize why we see so few people of color on these networks or working behind-the-scenes in newsrooms in the first place.

For those that are quick to jump on the criticism bandwagon, do they first understand that rap music's foundation was a check on society? That it was a mechanism for the powerless to speak their mind? Do they understand a history of socially and politically conscious music that was designed to mobilize people?

Even today, this music is a reaction to emotions of anger, frustration and inequity of mostly young minority people surviving in a society where the pendulum of justice swings away from them most of the time. In attempts to curb some of the criticism against this form of expression, moves by Dr. Ben Chavis, Russell Simmons and even Rev. Al Sharpton were aimed at targeting the true culprits behind negative/misogynystic music—record labels and corporations.

Record Companies Profit from Hip-Hop

On May 3 [2007], Tamika Mallory of Sharpton's National Action Network led a March for Hip-Hop Decency in front of Sony, Universal Records and the Time Warner building in Manhattan. "We cannot allow people to use the concept of freedom of speech and censorship as a shield for those who seek to denigrate any members of our society," she explains. "Freedom of speech is critical to freedom but so is the re-

9

Explicit Lyrics Encourage Teen Sex

Sarah Knoploh

Sarah Knoploh is a writer at the Culture and Media Institute in Alexandria, Virginia.

Recent studies show that teens who are exposed to music with lyrics that are sexually explicit are much more likely to have sex. Sexual lyrics that border on the pornographic and are degrading to women are easily accessible to children and teens. Many reviewers of these songs are as irresponsible as the artists because they ignore the inappropriate aspects of the lyrics but praise the artists' creativity. Drugs, alcohol, and profanity also are frequently mentioned in songs that teens listen to. Like the sex described in many songs, the lyrics that mention drugs and alcohol never discuss the need to act responsibly or explore the consequences of any actions.

Sex, alcohol, drugs, and profanity are easy to find: just turn on the radio. During the summer of 2009, the top 20 songs were full of such references. One hit song was even entitled "Birthday Sex."

Popular singer Lady Gaga's single "Love Game" was all about her sexual desires. The music video was so provocative, perhaps because of lesbians kissing, that it was banned in Australia. Another popular song, "Best I Ever Had" featured "f***" 19 separate times.

---

sponsibility that comes with it. We are not saying that rappers or anyone cannot speak in any manner they choose. We are saying that record and media companies shouldn't support it if it crosses the line of sexism, racism and homophobia."

Sounds like a wonderful idealistic thought without a doubt, except for the fact that these companies and media outlets have profited countless billions off the backs of rappers, hip-hop culture and the community. It's incredibly difficult for artist/groups with positive or socially conscious messages like a Dead Prez to get signed, and if they do, never will they see radio spins or record sales like their negative counterparts.

In an industry where marketing and radio promotion departments ensure that only certain albums get proper financial backing to guarantee air play and press, many talented people simply get shelved. Radio stations themselves have specific daily play lists, in effect brainwashing the masses with the same songs and the same messages.

Record Companies Limit Rappers

I've had rappers straight out tell me that they wanted to go with a specific single from their album but were forced to go with something else. And others have simply said they put out a single about women and money to reel in listeners to a deeper, profound meaning on the album that might otherwise have been ignored. Interesting isn't it?

These days Don Imus is at his ranch contemplating his next move. Chances are he'll return to the airwaves in some capacity in little time, while the young woman or man using music as a means to escape the all but insurmountable obstacles set in her/his path will find it ever more difficult because the world is now watching with keen eyes.

For those who are new to this genre of poetic expression, I suggest watching the new Bruce Willis/Queen Latifah documentary, "Hip-Hop Project." It beautifully captures the essence of what this culture was, is and should be about. Until critics begin to fully comprehend the many layers of hip-hop, its historical context and place in society, they should listen to what the Godfather of it all said to me the other day—the man who literally started hip-hop with two turntables—DJ Kool Herc: "Tell all the geniuses to back off of hip-hop. Leave hip-hop alone."

From June 10 to July 22 [2009], 29 songs were listed on the top 20 airplay charts as posted by Mediabase. An astonishing 69 percent of the songs made at least one reference to sex, alcohol, drugs, or contained profanity. Nearly half (46 percent) of the songs contained sexual lyrics and 31 percent of the songs referenced drugs or alcohol. Profanity occurred in 41 percent of the songs.

While just about everyone acknowledges that song lyrics are often inappropriate for children and teenagers, studies have shown that inappropriate lyrics can actually influence negative behavior in teenagers.

Despite these troubling numbers, the media has been generally indifferent to the obscenity, and often praised the artist. Some of the artists even performed on the networks' morning shows.

While just about everyone acknowledges that song lyrics are often inappropriate for children and teenagers, studies have shown that inappropriate lyrics can actually influence negative behavior in teenagers

Sexualized Lyrics Lead to Sexual Activity

Sex was a reoccurring theme in many of the songs, with some of the references very blatant. "Poker Face," sung by Lady Gaga included the lyrics, "And baby when it's love if it's not rough it isn't fun fun." In "Blame It" Jamie Foxx sings, "Now she got her hand on my leg. Got my seats all wet in my ride."

Dr. Brian A. Primack, of the University of Pittsburgh School of Medicine, conducted a study in 2009 in which he discovered that teenagers who listened to degrading and sexualized song lyrics were more likely to engage in sexual behavior. Primack stated, "In fact, exposure to lyrics describing degrading sex was one of the strongest associations with sexual activity. . . . These results provide further support for the need for additional research and educational intervention in this area."

Anybody listening to "Birthday Sex" would discover sex was all the song consisted of. The popular song made the charts for six weeks. Singer Jeremih left little to the imagination.

And make you wanna tell some-
body (body how I do)
Or maybe we can float on top my
waterbed
You close your eyes as I improve
between your legs
We work our way from kitchen
stoves and tables,
Girl, you know I'm only able to
please
Say you wanted flowers on the bed
But you got me and now it's on
again
Girl you know I-I-I, Girl you know
I-I-I
I been feenin,
Wake up in the late night
Been dreamin bout your loving,
girl
Girl you know I-I-I, Girl you know
I-I-I
Don't need candles and cake
Just need your body to make . . .
Birthday sex . . . Birthday sex
Birthday sex . . . Birthday sex

Some Ignore the Impact on Young People

But instead of reviewing the impact of Jeremih's song, Steve Jones of *USA Today* promoted the song and wrote, "'Birthday Sex' is proving to be a gift that keeps on giving for R & B newcomer Jeremih, whose salacious first single is one of the summer's hottest." He went on to write that it's "not bad for a self-taught musician." Jones also quoted Sean Ross of Edison Media Research, who said, "I think it would have been a hit any time."

On June 29, [2009,] Ken Capobianco, of the *Boston Globe*, gushed, "With his smash, steamy single 'Birthday Sex,' Jeremih almost single-handedly made everyone look forward to getting older. The debut from the Chicago native doesn't come close to capturing the magic of that small epiphany."

The media wasn't alone in rewarding Jeremih for "Birthday Sex." The Chicago public school system was so proud of the graduate's success that it enlisted him in a Twitter campaign to get Chicago teens back to school this fall [2009].

One song that was not quite as obvious in its sexual references was Britney Spear's "If You Seek Amy." It was only on the charts for two weeks, but when pronounced it spells "F*** me."

> Love me hate me, say what you
> want about me
> But all of the boys and all of the
> girls are begging to if you seek
> Amy
> Love me, hate me, but can't you see
> what I see?
> All of the boys and all of the girls
> are begging to if you seek Amy.

Pop music critic Ann Powers, of the *Los Angeles Times*, criticized Spears. She wrote, "The lyrics about Brittney as mannequin, sex object, paparazzi victim and leather-clad mistress have grown tedious. When the wittiest one is based around an adolescent text-message style joke, you know it's time to refocus."

Some Songs Should Be Banned

The Culture and Media Institute [CMI] previously reported about a radio station in Cincinnati that was considering banning the song from the airways. Q102's Patti Marshall told MTV, "we're publicly owned. . . . We have a responsibility to the public, you put this . . . out and act like we're all fuddy-duddies, like we're trying to make moral judgments. It's not about us. It's about the mom in the minivan with her eight-year-old."

The mom in the minivan might also want to think twice about playing Lady Gaga's hit song, "Love Game," which was on the charts for six weeks and made it to the number one spot. Lady Gaga sings about riding "a disco stick."

Let's have some fun, this beat is
sick
I wanna take a ride on your disco
stick
Don't think too much just bust
that stick
I wanna take a ride on your disco
stick

The song that was most degrading to women was "Right Round" by Flo Rida and featuring Keisha. On the charts for three weeks, the song is supposedly about a stripper.

Flo Rida was a popular guest on NBC's "Today Show." He appeared on July 24 [2009] during the "Today Talk" segment and on August 14 [2009], he performed for "Today's" summer concert series.

In an interview with DJ Boot, Flo Rida explained, "Hey, when I'm havin' a nice time in the club, you just might watch me make it rain. You might get some of my money. So I'm not really sayin' I don't want 'em to take my money, it's really that I've come to enjoy myself." But some of the lyrics in the chorus sound more like oral sex.

You spin my head right round,
right round

When you go down, when you go
down down

You spin my head right round,
right round

When you go down, when you go
down down

From the top of the pole I watch
her go down

She got me throwin' my money
around

Ain't nothing more beautiful to be
found

It's going down down

Drugs and Alcohol Are Also Condoned

Getting high and drunk seemed to be a popular topic for the singers in 2009. One song that referenced drugs was Kid Cudi's "Day 'n' Nite." He sang about getting high as, "the lonely stoner seems to free his mind at night." Jon Caramanica, of the *New York Times* described "Day 'n' Nite" as being, "somehow both viscous and zippy."

A total of 31 percent of the songs on the airplay charts referenced drugs or alcohol. But little has changed in two years; a study done in 2007 showed that one third of popular songs also referenced alcohol or drugs. A Reuters article featuring the study stated, "Most lyrical references to substance use were associated with partying, sex, violence and, or humor."

In "Blame It," by Jamie Foxx and featuring T-Pain, the singer assigns poor decisions to alcohol, completely abdicating personal responsibility.

Kelley L. Carter, of *USA Today*, did acknowledge that, "'Blame It' encourages listeners to chalk up bad decisions to an overindulgence of alcohol." But Carter went on to praise Foxx. "He can deliver award-worthy scenes with Hollywood's best, but he also can shake his rump next to today's hottest rappers and still come out garnering respect from both camps."

Blame it on the vodka, blame it on
the henny
Blame it on the blue tap, got you
feeling dizzy
Blame it on the a-a-alcohol
Blame it on the a-a-alcohol

Cursing Becomes the Norm

Many of the singers, it seemed, just couldn't resist peppering their songs with profanity. In the wildly popular song that made it to the top spot, "Boom Boom Pow," the Black Eyed Peas included profanity. They sang, "S***in' on y'all with the boom boom."

Profanity occurred in a total of 41 percent of the songs. The *Sacramento Bee* reported in 2008 that, "the Internet, television and other media may be making adolescents more comfortable with swearing, but it is their parents' own language habits that are the biggest influence." Parents are always the biggest influence, but obscenity in mainstream pop music clearly helps to normalize crude language.

The song that contained the most vulgar profanity was Drake's "Best I Ever Had." Not only did "f***" appear 19 times, but the song also included five other uses of profanity, including "the N word" three times, along with "s***" and "b****." A Youtube video of "Best I Ever Had" featured the lyrics uncensored with Drake's face as the backdrop. It was added in February and had over 16 million views at the end of July. CMI has previously reported that Youtube "remains a haven for soft-core pornography, obscenity and links to outside porn sites."

Parents are always the biggest influence, but obscenity in mainstream pop music clearly helps to normalize crude language.

Even with all the profanity, Chris Lee, of the *Los Angeles Times*, praised Drake's single as being, "not only a hit, but arguably 2009's 'Song of the Summer.'" He went on to write, "the song is an earnest expression of admiration from a young man to the object of his desire. And despite the coarseness of its explicit lyrics, 'Best I Ever Had' is surprisingly tender—at least, as emotive as hardcore hip-hop gets without being declared 'song.'"

"Best I Ever Had" only appeared that last week on the chart. The chorus includes:

I say you the f----- best

You the f-----best

You the f-----best

You the f-----best

You the best I eva had

Best I eva had

Best I eva had

Best I eva had

I said you the f----- in

Videos Leave Nothing to the Imagination

Hearing the lyrics is one matter, but music videos often go over the top in dramatizing them. All of the songs had music videos and 31 percent of the songs had music videos that were potentially offensive. Two of the music videos even had lesbians kissing: Black Eyed Peas "Boom Boom Pow" and Lady Gaga's "Love Game."

Lady Gaga had two music videos that were simply all about sex: "Poker Face" and "Love Game." "Love Game" was so offensive that, according to the *Daily Telegraph*, "Racy pop star Lady Gaga is too sexy for Australian TV censors, with her clip for 'Love Game' banned for 'frequent verbal and visual sexual references.'"

Australia was the first country to release "Love Game" and Video Hits producer Ben Fletcher stated, "It's pretty rare that we get a pop clip that's sexual to the point there's almost no way we can edit it without destroying the original content of the video."

The content of "Love Game" included suggestive dancing, with male dancers grabbing themselves at times. There was a scene with two lesbians kissing. In another scene one naked man and another man wearing only a top are sitting on a bench with a naked woman. In one shot the woman is leaning back into one man, spreading her legs in the air.

Lady Gaga's "Poker Face" also contained crude content, although in this music video she stuck to just kissing men. But it too had her and others dancing suggestively while barely dressed.

The most outlandish clip was from a 3 oh! 3's "Don't Trust Me" music video, which featured simulated bestiality.

No doubt many of these top songs are what teenagers are hearing on a daily basis, exposing themselves over and over to crude, obscene and nihilistic lyrics.

Very Few Positive Messages for Kids

With ipods, satellite radio, and music hotspots like Pandora, music is easy to obtain and has become an intricate part of daily life. In 2008, *Science Daily* cited a study that found 15–18 year olds listen to around 2.4 hours of music each day. No doubt many of these top songs are what teenagers are hearing on a daily basis, exposing themselves over and over to crude, obscene and nihilistic lyrics.

Some songs on the charts did feature positive messages. Nickelback's "If Today Was Your Last Day" and Miley Cyrus' "The Climb" both sent positive messages to teenagers. But more than two-thirds of songs had lyrics that promoted sexual activities, alcohol, and included profanity.

Explicit Lyrics Do Not Encourage Teen Sex

Carla Stokes, interviewed by Bonnie Zylbergold

Carla Stokes is a health educator specializing in the cultural and health dimensions of gender, media, and sexuality studies. Bonnie Zylbergold is assistant editor and senior writer for American Sexuality *magazine.*

Rap and hip-hop music can be used by young women to express themselves sexually. Many young people relate more easily to the themes found in hip-hop and rap, so the genres lend themselves to being used as a tool to teach girls about themselves, their gender, and their roles in society. The lyrics in these songs can initiate important and honest conversations about sex. Not all hip-hop and rap songs are sexist and misogynist. There are songs with more positive messages that do not get the same amount of airplay that songs with negative messages get.

Carla Stokes is an activist, researcher, and health educator specializing in the cultural and health dimensions of gender, media, and sexuality studies. The founding executive director of Helping Our Teen Girls In Real Life Situations, Inc. (HOTGIRLS), Dr. Stokes grew up during the golden age of hip-hop, when artists such as Run-DMC, LL Cool J, and Salt-N-Pepa achieved mainstream success. Dr. Stokes has pioneered methods of applying hip-hop and the Internet to uplift youth and girls of color in particular. She uses rap music lyrics and videos to educate young people about HIV/AIDS, sexuality, dating violence, and other social justice issues.

American Sexuality: How would you define hip-hop?

Carla Stokes: Well, there's a lot of debate about what hip-hop is, but it's a cultural movement that encompasses different elements including DJing, the art of MCing or rapping, break dancing, and graffiti art. Some even argue that hip-hop also includes activism, and that there's an element of hip-hop activism and social change within the culture.

On your website it says that you came of age at the same time hip-hop did. What was it about hip-hop music that inspired you to do what you do today?

I really think that hip-hop provides a unique space for girls to express themselves, specifically the girls that I work with, as well as young people in general. Historically speaking, it has provided a safe space for young people to speak out.

Girls Can Use Hip-Hop to Discuss Sex

That's interesting; a lot of people would argue the opposite.

Yeah, I should probably rephrase that: I think hip-hop provides a space, but not necessarily a safe space for women. But it has provided a space for young women to speak out about sexuality. That's how I became interested in hip-hop as a tool for education.

Especially since young people today are coming of age within hop-hop culture, hip-hop's become a significant way of fostering dialogue around many important issues they're facing in their lives.

Was there a specific female artist that inspired this realization?

Women have been integral to hip-hop culture from the very beginning. Ever since hip-hop came on the scene, women have had an important role in the genre. When I started working with young people, doing peer education around sexuality education, themes around rap music repeatedly came up in the classroom. And so I began using hip-hop as a tool, particularly rap music and music videos, to stimulate conversations about gender and sexuality. Especially since young people today are coming of age within hip-hop culture, hip-hop's become a significant way of fostering dialogue around many important issues they're facing in their lives. Plus, it's become a means of expression for the girls I work with who are using rap music to educate their peers on certain issues. There's a recording studio at the Boys & Girls Club we partner with and the girls have been recording songs that challenge how women are represented in both the media and youth oriented and cultural spaces.

When people tend to talk about hip-hop, much of the time they're focusing on the misogynistic and commercialized hip-hop music and are not really cognizant of the wide range of artists that are *addressing structural issues like sexism and racism.*

Positive Hip-Hop Songs Receive Less Attention

Overall, outside of the work you do, do you think that hip-hop and hip-hop culture has a positive or negative effect on youth?

I think it's complicated. There are contradictory messages in hip-hop. When people tend to talk about hip-hop, much of the time they're focusing on the misogynistic and commercialized hip-hop music and are not really cognizant of the wide range of artists that *are* addressing structural issues like sexism and racism. You know, those artists that are referred to as conscious hip-hop or rap artists. So there is a large positive movement; it's just not getting the same amount of attention or airplay on the radio.

Do you see a trend amongst the youth that you work with? Are they gravitating more toward one than the other?

Yeah. I work in the South, in Atlanta, Georgia, so the young people I work with aren't necessarily listening to the more socially conscious rappers. They do tend to listen to local hip-hop artists that may not be as progressive in their message. So I do see the trend toward listening to more commercialized hip-hop.

Teaching Girls to Empower Themselves

Speaking of commercial, what about pop stars like Brittney Spears? Do they fit in with your work?

They do in the sense that we use popular culture as an educational tool to spark discussions, and sometimes our conversations end up revolving around more mainstream artists. We had a conversation recently about the word *hot* and what it means, and discussed Paris Hilton's use of the word. Our activities do not revolve solely around hip-hop culture or rap music.

What about women referring to each other as bitch. *You hear it a lot; sometimes with a positive connotation, sometimes with a negative connotation, sometimes just as a friendly nickname between girls. What do you think about girls using the word amongst themselves, specifically within the communities you work with?*

We have this conversation with the girls in my program a lot and many are torn about it. Personally, I don't think that it's an empowering word, but I understand where some of the girls are coming from. Some of them have tried to redefine what *bitch* means but I still don't think that it's effective in the ways that they're using it. Very often, it's contradictory and hypocritical since the girls get upset when someone else calls them a bitch but continue calling other girls bitches too! It's complicated. . . .

Through her show, Tyra Banks has tried empowering young women, and she's very vocal about it. Could you remark on what she's currently doing?

I had a conversation with some family members about Tyra Banks, and I love Tyra. I do, I really like Tyra Banks! She has her TZONE camp for girls which focuses on self-esteem, and I appreciate many of the segments aired on the actual show. In fact, I've taped some of the episodes on body image and sexuality and plan to use them during some of the conversations that might come about in my workshops. I think Tyra evokes a dialogue that young women can relate to and, in so doing, a lot of girls look up to her as a role model.

African-American youth will turn to hip-hop music, an artist, or someone within their culture before they would potentially believe something that they hear on TV.

I found this question online: "Why is hip-hop sometimes called the CNN of black youth?" What is meant by this?

Chuck D famously said that rap music is the black CNN because rap music is the voice of black youth, who listen to and get information about a range of issues from rap music. They also consume a lot of media. In other words, hip-hop culture, and specifically music videos, are popular among black youth. Young people are more likely to listen to an artist they look up to, than say, CNN. African-American youth will turn to hip-hop music, an artist, or someone within their culture before they would potentially believe something that they hear on TV.

Some Reality Shows Encourage Stereotypes

What do you think about shows like Flavor of Love *and* I Love New York?

Personally, I just have issues with those shows. . . . I don't think that they . . . I sometimes watch them, but only for entertainment purposes and to stay in tune with what youth are watching. However, in terms of the messages perpetuated by these reality programs, they tend to demonize African-

American men as well as African-American women and African-American sexuality as a whole. So, no, I don't think the messages are particularly sexually healthy for the young women and men that tune in to watch them.

Actually, the girls brought it up not too long ago while we were working on our FIREGRL.com website; there's a section where three tiers of membership are offered depending on how much you participate on the website. The girls were debating about whether we should call the tiers Diamonds, Rubies, and Sapphires, and I began discussing the image of the Sapphire and how, according to black feminist scholars, the Sapphire represents the "loud mouthed black woman." And their immediate reaction was, *Oh, like New York.*

So, from what you can gather, the girls you work with also feel that this new slew of reality TV is negative.

They do, yes. But they still find entertainment value in it.

11

Rap and Hip-Hop Music Promote Violence

Geoff Schumacher

Geoff Schumacher writes for the Las Vegas Review-Journal. *He is the* Review-Journal's *director of community publications.*

Music lyrics, as well as movies and video games, glorify and encourage violence, materialism, and misogyny. Young people are attracted to and influenced by the romanticized view of "thug life," which leads them to try to imitate these lifestyles, often with violent results. Censorship is not the answer; it is not the role of government to restrict the constitutional right to freedom of speech. However, it is imperative that parents teach children about the dangers and limitations of the views of gangster rappers. The involvement of the Christian Right sometimes does more harm than good because it concentrates less on gun violence and more on sexual content.

My hard-earned reputation as a left-winger may be called into question today as I reveal a distinctly conservative aspect to my world view.

It turns out I'm in general agreement with old fogies and Christian groups that condemn those elements of the entertainment media that glorify violence and denigrate women.

Furthermore, I believe movies, music lyrics and video games that idealize the so-called "thug life" influence some young people to imitate the actions they hear about on their iPods or see on the screen.

I saw a fine film the other day, the Oscar-winning "Juno," but I left the theater thinking about a preview for an upcoming movie about teenage fighting called "Never Back Down."

This flick is about kids who fight for fun, presumably to spice up the monotony of modern suburban life. The main character is a kid who unwittingly attends a party where these fights occur, and proceeds to get his butt royally kicked by the recognized local champ of backyard fisticuffs. Meanwhile, the other kids at the party crowd around and cheer.

Rather than finding new friends, the defeated boy decides to undergo some martial arts training to become a better fighter so he can go back and get revenge on the tough guy who humiliated him.

It's entirely possible the Hollywood ending to this movie will suggest that bare-knuckle brawling is a poor excuse for a pastime, and that teenage boys would be better off walking barefoot on the beach with their girlfriends. But for many young viewers, the bloody fight scenes will be what they remember, and some of them may want to replicate what they see in the theater.

Is there no sense of responsibility that accompanies the quest for profit?

My question is this: Knowing what we all know about the prevalence of youth violence, crime and delinquency in this country, what self-respecting studio head green-lighted this movie? Is there no sense of responsibility that accompanies the quest for profit?

The same question should be asked of music companies that produce CDs by gangster rappers who sing about shooting people, dealing drugs and treating women like prostitutes. The claim that these performers are simply reflecting life on the mean streets of urban America is, for 90 percent of the material, a joke. Most of it's not art, it's commerce.

The same question should be asked of video game producers who create games in which players, operating in a very realistic-looking digital environment, have free rein to shoot police officers, innocent bystanders and anyone else who gets in the way of achieving a high score. These games appeal to our basest instincts.

Besides coarsening the culture, these forms of media influence some kids to act in destructive ways. Unlike many of my liberal brethren, I refuse to casually brush aside the evidence that media influence behavior. It happens in positive and negative ways, and we all know it.

It may not be possible to directly link violence-glorifying media to the recent shootings near Palo Verde High School and Gibson Middle School. But the fact that these teenage boys were carrying around loaded handguns and had no qualms about putting them to use on public streets strongly suggests "thug life" influences in their lives.

Here is where I part ways with some conservatives—and even some liberals—on this issue: I am not suggesting in any way, shape or form that the government should get involved in censoring movies, music or video games. Our First Amendment rights are very clear and should not be infringed. Neither the right nor the left should be trying to legislate freedom of speech.

But this constitutional right means we also are free to speak out against these media creations, and we are free to boycott them as well. We parents have every right to tell our kids these items are not welcome in our homes. Sadly, a whole lot of us are not drawing or enforcing these lines now.

· Unfortunately, most Americans who may agree with me on this issue do not bother to speak up, and those who do tend to hamper the cause more than help it. For example, last month a Texas-based group called Teen Mania Ministries held a rally in Times Square in New York City to protest explicit language and imagery in music, film, etc. Rebecca Bjerke, a

21-year-old participant, explained to a reporter why she was there: "To just stand up and say, 'We're tired of all the filth.' . . . You know, music and songs that are constantly so negative—just making us numb to the abuse of alcohol and drugs and sex and pornography and all that kind of stuff."

For many of us, it's not about biblical beliefs or prudish notions of morality, it's about people getting killed.

The problem is not these well-meaning kids in Times Square. The problem for the movement is that it's almost always Christian-based. Fundamentalist ministers and born-again believers lead the attack, and typically focus first on sexual issues, not gun violence. Other people alarmed by the dangerous effects of irresponsible media don't want to be associated with the Christian right's crusades.

For many of us, it's not about biblical beliefs or prudish notions of morality, it's about people getting killed.

Juan Williams, well-known correspondent for National Public Radio and political analyst for Fox News, wrote a book in 2006 called "Enough," in which he examines the political and cultural issues holding back black America. Williams condemns the worst elements of rap music and chides African-American leaders, and black women in particular, for not speaking out against it.

"The consequence of black leaders failing to speak out against the corruption of rap for all those years resulted in real damage to the most vulnerable of black America—poor children, boys and girls, often of broken homes," Williams writes. "As a group, they were desperately searching for black pride in a sea of images being thrown at them on TV, on the radio, on the Internet, and in advertising. What those children found was a larger-than-life rapper who was materialistic, sexist and violent, and used the word 'nigger' as a casual description of all black people. It was a musical minstrel show that would have been a familiar delight to 19th century slave owners."

The Palo Verde and Gibson shootings have generated (mostly) healthy discussion in the community about causes and solutions. There is not one cause or one solution. But it is possible to identify several probable causes and start exploring ways to address them, if not solve them.

Entertainment media of the types discussed here are one cause, I believe. And the solution, in part, is for a wider spectrum of the public to recognize the toxic nature of this dreck and refuse to support it.

We parents must develop a better understanding of the difference between "No Country for Old Men" and teen flicks that depict sadism and revenge as cool. We need to draw a clearer distinction between music of artistic value and the misogynist ravings of Snoop Dogg. We need to understand that for some 12-year-old boys, untold hours playing dehumanizing, violent video games just might have an effect on the way they deal with the real world.

And you don't have to be a Baptist preacher to complain about it.

Rap and Hip-Hop Music Reveal but Do Not Promote Violence

Yan Dominic Searcy

Yan Dominic Searcy is an associate professor of social work and sociology at Chicago State University.

Rap music is often accused of being responsible for many of society's problems because of its emphasis on sex, drugs, and violence. It's simplistic to lay the blame for all problems, such as teenage pregnancy and gun violence, entirely at the feet of rap and hip-hop musicians. These problems existed before the advent of rap and hip-hop; the music only mirrors life. Changing the lyrics found in these songs will not change society. Society will only change when people work to change the way things are.

Hip-hop has taken its lumps, but like any great fighter, it takes its punishment and keeps stepping forward. The latest round brings Bill Cosby and Alvin Poussaint into the ring, brandishing their book, "Come On People: On the Path From Victims to Victors." The book argues that blacks should reclaim their communities by placing family, education and economic upward mobility first. That is a noble position. It's unsettling, however, that Cosby and Poussaint suggest rap music "promotes the moral breakdown of the family."

Displaying a lack of understanding of both the music and the complexity of social problems, the authors jab by stating without proof that hip-hop "deliberately influences women to become pregnant before they have finished their education and influences men to shuck their responsibilities when this happens."

And FoxSports.com columnist Jason Whitlock, in writing about the November 2007 shooting death of NFL player Sean Taylor, had this to say: "Our self-hatred has been set to music.... I blame hip-hop for playing a role in the genocide of American black men."

At first glance, there appears to be a certain logic to the claim that young people, particularly young blacks, can be influenced enough by rap music to carry out any criminal and violent messages.

But if that were true, it should follow that if the music is changed, the results will be different.

This line of reasoning led Cosby to record a rap album, "Cosby Narratives Vol. 1: State of Emergency," set for release in the coming weeks. Cosby will not rap himself, but the album will trumpet the same themes of responsibility, education and building self-esteem that appear in his recent book.

Many rappers grew up amid violence, police harassment, poverty, drugs and promiscuity. Rappers will tell you they rap about what they know. If the community wants to change rap lyrics, the community must change reality.

Hip-Hop Music Does Not Cause Violence

Rap, however, makes too easy a target. And writers such as Cosby, Poussaint and Whitlock confound the true sources of the social problems they lament. Some people who listen to rap music may engage in violent behavior and sexual promiscuity, but the music is not the cause.

Instead, as has been observed many times—including routinely by rappers themselves—hip-hop music reflects reality.

Many rappers grew up amid violence, police harassment, poverty, drugs and promiscuity. Rappers will tell you they rap about what they know. If the community wants to change rap lyrics, the community must change reality.

Jazz and Blues Lyrics Are Sexually Explicit

But beyond that familiar argument lies a historical context that hip-hop critics overlook. Long-celebrated forms of African-American music, such as jazz and blues, have always been sprinkled with sexuality and measures of violence. Granted, rap music is more lyrically explicit. But sexual double-entendre has been used for nearly a century in jazz and blues.

For example, jazz pioneer Jelly Roll Morton was not exactly named after a pastry. Scantily clad showgirls were staples of the big-band era. Ella Fitzgerald recorded "Bewitched, Bothered and Bewildered" in 1956. She sang of being "oversexed again" and observed, "Horizontally speaking, he's at his very best."

It should not be forgotten that rock 'n' roll, a musical form created by blacks, was originally a slang term for sex.

Granted, rap music is more lyrically explicit. But sexual double-entendre has been used for nearly a century in jazz and blues.

There is another reason to look back. Violence and crime appear to be increasing at alarming rates. But interestingly—and fortunately—the city of Chicago has not surpassed the record for most murders in one year. The record was established in 1974 at 970 murders (nearly 800 victims were black).

Would it be safe to assume that R&B music was lyrically violent at the time?

On the contrary, love and sex were the themes of the day. Among the chart-topping R&B singles were "Superstition," by Stevie Wonder; "Could It Be I'm Falling in Love?" by the Spinners; "Love Train," by the O'Jays; and "Let's Get It On," by Marvin Gaye.

Based on the Cosby-Poussaint analysis, the 1970s should have been love-filled, not murder-filled. Just as soul music did not make people love more then, rap music does not make people kill more now. Listening to John Coltrane does not make people do heroin.

In 2007 the murder rates in New York (the birthplace of hip-hop) and Chicago (hometown of Kanye West) decreased to levels unseen since the 1960s. This is even more noteworthy given that firearms are far more prevalent and powerful today than years ago. A study released in 2006 by Franklin Zimring of the University of California, Berkeley, found that crime rates across all major cities declined in the "gangsta rap" 1990s to levels more closely resembling those of the big-band era.

And counter to the Cosby and Poussaint assertions, unwed teen pregnancy rates are lower now than in the 1970s.

Not only do critics of hip-hop eschew statistical data when mounting attacks, some selectively use race to defend their positions while ignoring it when it fails to support them.

Predominantly white communities are not occupied by tacitly accepted open-air drug markets, police brutality, unevenly distributed justice and families enduring the legacy of economic oppression and subjugation.

The Reality for Many Blacks Is Violence

For example, most hip-hop consumers are white. So following the logic of the writers, there should be an abundance of violence among whites who mimic what they hear.

Does the fact that many whites do not mimic the violence mean whites are somehow immune to the lyrics? Or is it that their daily life realities are not littered with poor-performing schools, a lack of extracurricular activities and limited job opportunities stemming from postindustrial economic changes? Predominantly white communities are not occupied by tacitly accepted open-air drug markets, police brutality, unevenly distributed justice and families enduring the legacy of economic oppression and subjugation.

Such social problems are complex. Yet certain critics find it easier to lash out at a 23-year-old rapper wearing bling and a video showing bathing suit–clad beauties than to take on public officials who continually underfund public education. It also is easier to chastise a rapper for his depiction of violence than to challenge the National Rifle Association and support bans on assault rifles or handguns.

Hip-hop music does merit criticism, and I should admit that I am critical. I dislike cliched videos and subject matter, abysmal live performances and current songs that trumpet being a street soldier yet neglect commenting on the war in Iraq.

The ills of the black community, however, cannot be placed squarely on the shoulders of hip-hop music. Faced with problems that lack easy solutions, people often look for scapegoats. In this case, the scapegoat is hip-hop music.

If America wants to change rap lyrics, America must change the realities that inspire those lyrics.

Racist and Sexist Rap Lyrics Must Be Rejected by African Americans

Anthony Asadullah Samad

Anthony Asadullah Samad is the managing director of the Urban Issues Forum, a national columnist, and author of Saving the Race: Empowerment Through Wisdom.

The furor over Don Imus's comments about black female basketball players at Rutgers University should lead to some introspection on the part of the African American community with regard to similar words that can be found in many rap and hip-hop songs. Claiming that any control of offensive lyrics is a form of censorship is a fragile argument. The right to free speech does not include encouraging violence and promiscuity and humiliating another person. Rappers and hip-hop musicians who use violent and degrading lyrics must be educated as to why they are contributing to racism and sexism in America. It is unacceptable for them to claim that they are only describing certain women and not referring to all women.

The door of intolerance to racially offensive commentary shut pretty quickly on Don Imus last week. As quickly as he replied to his producer's "tough hos" comments with a "nappy headed hoes" follow-up, activists and opinion leaders piled on with a feeding frenzy reminiscent of a hog call at dinner time.

Anthony Asadullah Samad, "Imus, Repentant and Fired—Rappers, Unrepentant and Uninspired: Now Comes the Real Challenge," *Chicago Defender*, vol. 101, no. 197, April 20—22, 2007, p. 8. Copyright © 2007 by Anthony Asadullah Samad. All rights reserved. Used with the permission of the *Chicago Defender*.

Imus was mush by the end of the feeding and repentant and fired from both his media groups (NBC and CBS).

In the dialogue, however, was a conversation about how the Black community could be so unforgiving with Imus' language, but so unscrutinizing about the lyrics of dozens of rappers that use the same language. A whole lot of people have been waiting for the door to crack on this conversation about degrading rap lyrics.

I thought it would happen last year when "It's Hard Out Here For A Pimp" won an Oscar.

However, Black people were so obviously conflicted (happy or shocked) that the real conversation about what the song was really saying never took place. But it's taking place now and the rappers are already on the defensive (or offensive, depending on how you look at it).

Lyrics that incite violence, promote rape and other hypersexual activities, and for degrading the humanity of a person or any group of people is not covered under free speech.

Not Part of Free Speech

Russell Simmons, whom I have a great deal of respect for, is advancing his "regulating rap could lead to censorship" argument. The "free speech" cry is an argument that comes up and the call to regulate radio and television stations that use public airwaves to promote offensive lyrics. Lyrics that incite violence, promote rape and other hyper-sexual activities, and for degrading the humanity of a person or any group of people is not covered under free speech.

Public ignorance allowed most to believe that this is "protected (free) speech," but nothing that disrupts the public order, or endangers the public is covered under free speech. Vulgarity and extreme verbal assault is a permitted restriction or unprotected (as Imus found out), so we really ought to stop allowing rappers to hide behind the free speech shield. Then there are those who don't get it at all.

The unrepentant rappers who either don't understand what they're doing to open the door of hatred and racial casting of African Americans, or in acting as true capitalist mercenaries that put money before everything—don't care about the racial backlash created when they "keep it real."

Vulgarity and extreme verbal assault is a permitted restriction or unprotected ..., so we really ought to stop allowing rappers to hide behind the free speech shield.

Just as Bad When Blacks Say It

For instance, when they asked Snoop Dogg about his use of the language that Imus got fired for, his response was that he's not talking about all women when he uses the word, "just the ghetto hos." Uh huh.

I'm sure that when Imus conversation started out saying that the Rutgers girls had tattoos ... tough demeanor ... and of course, nappy hair ... his inference was that they were from the rough side of town, or as Snoop would call them, "ghetto hos."

What's the difference here? There is none. And for the past 20 years, there has been a constant twisting, even defending, of this type of irrational justification.

Before there was "shock jocks," there was "shock rap." But shock rap, the so-called "keeping it real" street life, like "shock" talk radio to follow, have only been able to attack the despised and defenseless.

When rap attacked the powerful and complicit, it was repulsed and restricted. Ice T's "Cop Killer" and Public Enemy's "Who's Criminal" are just two instances of rappers who tried to attack police and political corruption on the airwaves, only to have their music "censored" as not in the public interest.

Twelve years ago, a group in Los Angeles (of which I was a part) waged a series of protests and boycotts against radio stations that played music with the words, "n----," "*itch" or "ho" in the lyric.

One station, which is now out of business, was recalcitrant in complying with the community's desire to take these songs off the radio, and even used Black people to defend the station's policy (the free speech argument) and even used the airwaves to personally attack activists (including myself) calling for the elimination of offensive lyrics in rap music.

What followed was [that] the radio stations colluded with the record companies and began running "promos" thanking 92.3 "The Beat" (I can call their name because they're no longer in existence) for "Keeping it real—fo' shizzle, my nizzels" (rap code for "for sure, my n----s").

Competition (for audience ratings) being what it was, once one station started playing gutter rap, they all started playing it. Everything went downhill from there.

Teach Young Rappers to Change

Now, we're looking at a whole generation of rappers that came of age in the late 1990s and early 2000s from Jay Z to 50 Cent to The Game and some I probably don't even know that are more raw than the generation before them. And more successful.

We'd be foolish to think rappers are going to leave all that money on the table to restore "Black dignity" in rap music. Yet, that's what we're asking them (and expecting them) to do.

The community is trying to reject the stigmas of racism and genocide at the same time.

Like the Don Imus situation, it will be a lot easier to shut down the record companies and programmers than these rappers. They don't understand the genocide that they've become host to. They think it's just music, or just a song.

The real challenge now is to help the rappers know better. That's where we are now in the discussion, to convince a generation (maybe two) that they're not n----s, pimps and hos, and it's going to take plenty "piling on."

Like the kind that got Imus fired last week. And the kind that makes us get on the same page on this vulgar lyrics tip.

Consumers of All Races Should Boycott Offensive Rap Music

Justin D. Ross

Justin D. Ross is a member of the Maryland House of Delegates. He is a Democrat who represents Prince George's County.

There's been a lot of debate within the African American community about hip-hop and the extent to which its lyrics are responsible for sexually demeaning and humiliating women; however, there also should be the same debate within the white community because whites actually buy the greatest amount of rap and hip-hop music. Whites listen to rap music that glorifies violence and sex and enables stereotypes to continue. This is causing whites to become numb to the very real problems that occur in many African American communities. All races should stop consuming rap music.

When it comes to sexism and racism in hip-hop, I'm part of the problem.

Let me explain. I love hip-hop—have ever since it first came on the scene when I was in elementary school. Over the years, I've bought hundreds of tapes, CDs and downloads, gone to countless rap concerts, even worn my favorite artists' clothing lines. We used to think of hip-hop as just a black thing, but it's not. The largest share of rap music sales in America goes to white listeners. That would be me.

So I'm not just sounding off when I say this: It's time for a boycott of all rap music that stereotypes African Americans or insults and degrades women. And in particular, the people who need to be doing the boycotting are white fans like myself.

It's time for a boycott of all rap music that stereotypes African Americans or insults and degrades women. And in particular, the people who need to be doing the boycotting are white fans like myself.

Whites Should Eschew Offensive Music

In the current debate over whether hip-hop has become degrading to women and harmful to race relations, I've heard quite a bit from black activists, some of whom have fought for years against the sort of lyrics I'm writing about, and I've gotten several earfuls from black rap artists. But I haven't heard a peep from the white fans who essentially underwrite the industry by purchasing more than 70 percent of the rap music in this country, according to Mediamark Research Inc. I don't presume to tell any artist, studio executive or record label what to record or not record. But I will presume to ask young white customers: Why are we buying this stuff?

Across the country, white kids in comfortable suburban neighborhoods (mine was Greenbelt [Maryland]) sit in their cars or bedrooms or studio apartments, listening to the latest rap music that glorifies violence, peddles racist stereotypes and portrays women as little more than animals. We look through the keyhole into a violent, sexy world of "money, ho's and clothes." We're excited to be transported to a place where people brag about gunplay, use racial epithets continually and talk freely about dealing drugs. And then we turn off whatever we're listening to and return to our comfy world in time for dinner.

But music is powerful. You can't just turn it on and off with a switch. Back in 1989, rap music had this white kid wearing a leather African pendant and reading Malcolm X because Chuck D did. Before I graduated from Kenmoor Middle School, I was ready to "Fight the Power" because Public Enemy told me to (even though I didn't really know what that meant).

But it has been a long time since Public Enemy. Some hip-hop artists (the Roots, Talib Kweli, D.C.'s own Wale) still succeed without using stereotypes and misogyny, but too much of today's rap goes another way: It's full of drug dealing and killing, and it portrays women as sex objects. A generation ago, at least some element of hip-hop remained loyal to the civil rights movement. Now songs talk so casually about selling crack and committing murder that listeners are desensitized to the words' effect.

Whites Desensitized to Black Violence

Let's be clear about what we—rap's huge white audience—are becoming insensitive to: crime against black people, drugs being sold in black neighborhoods, black people being killed. I think this desensitization is partly responsible for the absence of discussion about the cruel fact that, according to a 2001 study by the Department of Health and Human Services, the leading killer of African Americans ages 15 to 34 is homicide. It may also help explain why you'll seldom hear politicians talking about another awful statistic: According to the same study, African Americans are five times more likely than whites to be victims of homicide.

So who are the rappers really aiming at? Many rap songs use the "N-word" a dozen times or more. But I can count on two hands the number of times I've heard the words "whitey" or "cracker" in rap music. I wonder: If the Grand Wizard [of the Ku Klux Klan] himself owned a record label, how much different would the music sound?

I also wonder what would happen if rap artists started talking about selling dope in the suburbs, or shooting white people or beating down white men. Would rap's comfortable white fans continue to consume it? I suspect the record companies wouldn't even sell it. Like the majority of people who buy rap music, the majority of people who get rich off it are white. That sort of thing might hit a little too close to home for hip-hop's fans and profiteers.

Let's be clear about what we—rap's huge white audience—are becoming insensitive to: crime against black people, drugs being sold in black neighborhoods, black people being killed.

The other day, my 3-year-old wanted to listen to some music on my iPod. Before I let her, I checked out what I had on there. Much of it was trash I wouldn't let her listen to. I've been waxing intellectual for years about the state of rap and how it needs to change, and there I was, looking at my iPod and seeing songs such as "Hustlin'," "Bury Me a G" and "Poppin' My Collar," all of which are guilty of the very offenses I just decried and all of which I purchased within the past year.

That's when it hit me: I'm the problem. It's time for me and others like me to own up to our role in peddling degrading hip-hop. Of course, I can't legislate a boycott of offensive rap, except for myself. And that's exactly what I plan to do.

Music Censorship Threatens Cultural Growth and Survival in Somalia

Jessica Saxton

Jessica Saxton studies mass communication and music at the Queensland University of Technology in Australia. She is a contributor to Not Street Press, *a Brisbane-based music blog, as well as to the* AU Review, *an Australian online publication.*

The government of Somalia is so threatened by the potential of music to unify people and ignite their passions that it has completely removed music from the radio. The government's argument is that music only distracts from prayer and destroys Islamic beliefs; however, music always has allowed people to express themselves creatively. Banning music strips people of their individuality and their right to self-expression. Such censorship in the name of religious extremism is an issue of power. Clamping down on the right of people to listen to, as well as to make, music is a tool to break the will of the people.

The Somali press has been heavily censored since 1969; in the last 40 years many newspapers have been shut down, journalists imprisoned and media stations smothered beneath stifling government control. Now musicians are fleeing the country for fear of being beaten, imprisoned or killed for their art.

Hezb al-Islam leader Sheik Mohamed Ibrahim told AFP that the ban was an appropriate move in an attempt to stop "evil deeds". It now seems in the extremist governed, southern regions of Somalia, listening to music is illegal. Practicing music is illegal. Killing in the name of religion is commonplace: yet the airwaves remain music-free to save their souls.

The country's politics are divided geographically; the northern regions of Puntland and Somaliland are under the 'national government' known as the TFG, while areas south of Puntland are predominantly under extremist control, largely Al Shabaab. From the Garowe Radio Station, operating out of Puntland, Mohammed Omar Dahla says many people in the areas under Al Shabaab rule are afraid to play music in their own homes.

In the extremist-governed regions, the only resemblance to music is the approved Nasheed; which is simply religious chanting. Even jingles have been banned from radio. According to militants, the playing of music violates core Islamic principles and distracts from worship. Music worldwide has long been seen as a means of worship, storytelling and creative expression. Perhaps this is why it is such a dangerous weapon.

Music worldwide has long been seen as a means of worship, storytelling and creative expression. Perhaps this is why it is such a dangerous weapon.

Music Deprivation Engenders Despair

A Somali journalist, Kassim Mohamed, says the people are becoming depressed from the sound of gunfire every day, "I think without music they are not going to survive." The ban on music includes jingles; as such, sound effects on the air have largely become animal noises and the sound of gunfire. Kassim is fearful that many people, especially youths, who formerly would be playing or listening to music, will find ulterior, less desirable means to cure their boredom. It is also possible that with the only media input being religious chants, news and below-par sound effects, their cultural growth could be significantly stifled.

The Somali Arts and Culture Foundation (SAAC) have strongly condemned the ban. The deterioration of musical expression in extremist-controlled areas mean musicians, composers and artists are facing daily threats and joblessness. They have pleaded with the Shabaab groups who initiated the ban to reconsider, to no avail.

In the capital Mogadishu, it is not only quiet on the air. The National Theatre, once considered one of the most beautiful theatres in Africa, and nearly all other places where the Somali artists used to perform their music, have been forced to close down. Many are now derelict and broken, housing the homeless alongside animals.

Exiles Sing to Express Pain

Many musicians have fled Somalia, fearful of punishment for their art. Living in exile in Kenya since childhood, a group of Somali musicians formed an anti-extremist rap group, Waayaha Cusub. They sing of the corruption and repression of their home. Since their formation in 2004, they have recorded albums on pirated CD's and DVD's, their lyrics blatant attacks on the Somali warlord's actions.

They highlight the hypocrisy of the rule in extremist regions and defend that practicing music does not make them 'bad Muslims'. "We pray five times a day. We go to the mosque, we fast. But we don't steal and we don't kill." Some of Waayaha Cusub's CD's have made their way back to Somalia, where they are eagerly received, to be played in secret. An underground rebellion; simply listening to the music is an act against the Shabaab rule. It may not seem like much to listen to a CD, but what it means is the power of music has reinfiltrated the southern regions of Somalia. Though it is not being freely aired, the ideas expressed in the music are being spread and kept alive within the people. It's a sign that the Somali people are not ready to take this cultural repression lying down, they are still capable of independent thought and their own ideals, though stemming from the same religion, are not that of their current political leaders.

Omar's station is based in Garowe, the capital of Puntland, where he says there is no Shabaab. Radios play national and international music freely, without fear of extremist reaction.

It may not seem like much to listen to a CD, but what it means is the power of music has re-infiltrated the southern regions of Somalia.

"If there is any Shabaab, he is shot on sight or arrested by the government troops. So in Puntland music plays all day everyday on more than 16 independent radio stations across the State."

Revolution or Loss of Identity

Hezb al-Islam says they are striving to eliminate 'evil deeds'. People in Somalia are killed, punished and culturally repressed daily. This is a blatant violation of the basic human right to self expression. Is that not an 'evil deed' in itself, far worse than music playing on the radio? In my discussions with Omar, he mused over the ban's moral contradictions.

"No, Shabaab is not in Somalia to 'stop evil deeds,'" he said. "Simply, they want power. You can try to avoid that basic principle, and focus on music bans, and so on, but Shabaab want power. And power is earned in two ways; fear or respect. For Shabaab, its only option is fear."

Music's ability to unite, uplift and inspire people is ever more powerful than the repression that can be attained through fear. "You can never stop the Somali people from listening to music because it is part of their culture," said former renowned musician, Mohamed Omar Dalha in a recent press release.

Music's ability to unite, uplift and inspire people is even more powerful than the repression that can be attained through fear.

With musicians fleeing, and working on protest music from outside extremist control, individuals within the country secretly listening to CD's and the northern half still operating freely, it looks as if the repression will end in two ways. Either the extremist-controlled areas will lose their cultural identity and will to operate independently, or the people will rise against their repressors in a renaissance that will either evacuate the affected regions or revolutionise them.

Organizations to Contact

The editors have compiled the following list of organizations concerned with the issues debated in this book. The descriptions are derived from materials provided by the organizations. All have publications or information available for interested readers. The list was compiled on the date of publication of the present volume; the information provided here may change. Be aware that many organizations take several weeks or longer to respond to inquiries, so allow as much time as possible.

American Family Association (AFA)
PO Drawer 2440, Tupelo, MS   38803
(622) 844-5036 • fax: (662) 842-7798
website: www.afa.net

Founded in 1977, AFA represents and supports traditional family values, focusing primarily on the influence of television and other media on society. Though it does not support censorship, AFA advocates responsibility and accountability of the entertainment industry. The association believes that through its various products, the entertainment industry has played a major role in the decline of those values on which our country was founded and which keep a society and its families strong and healthy. AFA publishes a monthly newsletter and the *AFA Journal*.

Artists Without Frontiers (AWF)
PO Box 35460, London   NW8 9YF
   UK
+44 (0) 207 443 79 09
e-mail: info@artistswithoutfrontiers.com

Artists Without Frontiers is a nonprofit group devoted to promoting cultural and intellectual understanding among artists, creating a community of artists to increase awareness of the importance of the role of art in the world, and defending the arts against such threats as censorship. The group works to bring together artists with seminars, workshops, and exhibitions; supports human rights; and researches the needs and problems of new artists. The *AWF Magazine* is its online publication.

Concerned Women for America (CWA)
1015 Fifteenth St. NW, Suite 1100, Washington, DC   20005
(202) 488-7000 • fax: (202) 488-0806
website: www.cwfa.org

CWA is a public policy women's organization devoted to bringing Christian principles to public policy. CWA concentrates on the core issues of the family, the sanctity of human life, religious freedom, education, pornography, and national sovereignty. The group's publications include the monthly magazine *Family Voice*.

Culture and Media Institute (CMI)
325 S. Patrick St., Alexandria, VA   22314
(703) 683-9733 • fax: (703) 683-9736
e-mail: contact.cmi@mediaresearch.org
website: www.mrc.org/cmi/

The Culture and Media Institute was established to protect and help restore America's culture, traditional values, character, and morals from the liberal media. It works to ensure that social conservatives and religious believers are portrayed fairly in the media. The cultural division of the Media Research Center, CMI is committed to correcting misconceptions about religious faith and social conservatism in the media. It publishes *Eye on Culture* articles on its website.

Freemuse
Nytorv 17, 3rd Floor, Copenhagen   DK-1450
  Denmark
+45 33 32 10 27

e-mail: freemuse@freemuse.org
website: www.freemuse.org

Freemuse is an independent international organization advocating freedom of expression for musicians and composers worldwide. It is membership based, with its secretariat based in Copenhagen, Denmark, and was formed at the first World Conference on Music and Censorship held in Copenhagen in November 1998. Its publications include *Headbanging Against Repressive Regimes, Human Rights for Musicians*, and *Music Will Not Be Silenced.*

Hip-Hop Association (H2A)

545 Eighth Ave., 10th Floor, New York, NY   10018
(718) 682-2744
e-mail: info@hiphopassociation.org
website: www.hiphopassociation.org

H2A is a nonprofit organization whose goal is to use hop-hop culture as a tool to facilitate critical thinking and foster social change and unity by empowering communities through the use of media, technology, education, and leadership development, while preserving hip-hop culture for future generations. It works to achieve this mission with learning and capacity-building tools, programming resources, and consulting services.

Index on Censorship

Free Word Centre, London   EC1R 3GA
   UK
+44 (0) 20 7324 2522
e-mail: enquirer@indexoncensorship.org
website: www.indexoncensorship.org

Founded in 1972 as a magazine, the Index on Censorship is a British organization devoted to supporting the right to freedom of expression. It promotes the freedom of expression via its website with information and news from around the world. It also publishes the *Index on Censorship* magazine.

National Association for the Advancement of Colored People (NAACP)

4805 Mr. Hope Dr., Baltimore, MD   21215
(877) 622-2798
website: www.naacp.org

The NAACP is a civil rights organization that works to ensure the political, educational, social, and economic equality of rights of all persons and to eliminate racial hatred and racial discrimination. It formed the STOP Campaign to combat demeaning images of African Americans in the media, particularly African American women, and conducted a mock funeral for the N-word in July 2007.

National Coalition Against Censorship (NCAC)

19 Fulton St., Suite 407, New York, NY   10038
(212) 807-6222 • fax: (212) 807-6245
e-mail: ncac@ncac.org
website: www.ncac.org

NCAC, founded in 1974, is an alliance of fifty-two national nonprofit organizations, including literary, artistic, religious, educational, professional, labor, and civil liberties groups. The coalition works to educate its members and the public at large about the dangers of censorship and how to oppose it. Its publications include *NCAC Censorship News* and *Censoring Culture: Contemporary Threats to Free Expression.*

Recording Industry Association of America (RIAA)

1025 F St. NW, 10th Floor, Washington, DC   20004
(202) 775-0101
website: www.riaa.org

RIAA is the trade group that represents the US recording industry, including protecting the First Amendment and intellectual property rights of artists and music labels. Its mission is to foster a business and legal climate that supports and promotes its members' creative and financial vitality. RIAA members create, manufacture, and distribute approximately 85 percent of all legitimate sound recordings produced and sold in the United States. The group publishes the *Fast Tracks* newsletter.

Bibliography

Books

Peter Blecha   *Taboo Tunes: A History of Banned Bands and Censored Songs.* San Francisco: Backbeat Books, 2004.

Michael Drewett, ed. *Popular Music Censorship in Africa.* Surrey, UK: Ashgate, 2006.

Jo Glanville, ed.   *Smashed Hits 2.0: Music Under Pressure.* Thousand Oaks, CA: Sage, 2010.

Raiford Guins   *Edited Clean Version: Technology and the Culture of Control.* Minneapolis: University of Minnesota Press, 2008.

Mickey Hess   *Is Hip-Hop Dead? The Past, Present, and Future of America's Most Wanted Music.* Santa Barbara, CA: ABC-CLIO, 2007.

Laudan Nooshin   *Music and the Play of Power in the Middle East, North Africa and Central Asia.* Surrey, UK: Ashgate, 2009.

Michael G. Plumides Jr. *Kill the Music: The Chronicle of a College Radio Idealist's Rock and Roll Rebellion in an Era of Intrusive Morality and Censorship.* Charleston, SC: Booksurge, 2009.

Annie J. Randall   *Music, Power, and Politics.* New York: Routledge, 2005.

Jonathan Ritter Jr., ed.	*Music in the Post-9/11 World.* New York: Routledge, 2007.
Anna Tomasino, ed.	*Music and Culture.* New York: Pearson Longman, 2005.

Periodicals

Firpo W. Carr	"Curse Words & Kemetic Culture," *Los Angeles Sentinel*, August 21–27, 2008.
William Jelani Cobb and Mary Dyson	"After the Verdict, Should We Continue Supporting R. Kelly?," *Ebony*, October 2008.
Johnnetta B. Cole	"What Hip-Hop Has Done to Black Women," *Ebony*, March 2007.
Robert Cooper	"Say No to Sexual Objectification Full Stop!," *New African*, October 2008.
Akua Djanie	"Music Videos or Porn with Music?," *New African*, March 2010.
James. M. Dorsey	"Rap and Metal on Planet Islam," *Reason*, December 2010.
Howard Gensler	"Simmons Issues Hip-Hop Language Rules," *Philadelphia Daily News*, April 24, 2007.
Bob Herbert	"Behind the Façade," *New York Times*, July 4, 2009.

Felicia R. Lee   "Protesting Demeaning Images in Media," *New York Times*, November 5, 2007.

Courtney E. Martin   "Pop Singer Makes Slaving for Beauty Look Ugly," *Women's eNews*, May 18, 2006.

Milwaukee Journal Sentinel   "Sex, Sex and More Sex. Got Your Attention?," August 10, 2008.

Shelly Palmer   "The Rap on Freedom of Speech," *Huffington Post*, April 27, 2007.

Pittsburgh Tribune-Review   "Cause for Reflection," February 9, 2008.

Cleveland Prince   "Hip Hop and Youth at Risk," *Judges' Journal*, Summer 2007.

Barbara Reynolds   "Black Leaders Silent as Black Rappers Create Environ of Death and Abuse," *Afro-American Red Star*, February 21–27, 2009.

Sarah Rodman   "Policing Rap Lyrics Is Near Impossible Task," *Boston Globe*, April 25, 2007.

Kelefa Sanneh   "How Don Imus's Problem Became a Referendum on Rap," *New York Times*, April 25, 2007.

Susan L. Taylor   "I Apologize," *Essence*, July 2007.

Amy Tuteur   "Don't Blame Me: The Sexually Degrading Lyrics Made Me Do It," *Salon*, February 26, 2009.

Cathy Young   "Enforcing Virtue: Is Social Stigma a
                     Threat to Liberty, or Is It Liberty in
                     Action?," *Reason* March 2007.

Index

Numerals

3OH!3 (singer duo), 65
50 Cent (rapper), 11, 36, 38–39, 52–53, 86

A

Abram, Malcolm X, 23–28
AC/DC (music group), 8
Activism, 43–44, 68
African Americans
    female exploitation, 45–50, 54
    genocide of, 79, 86–87
    Hip-hop lyrics and, 40–44, 76, 79
    racism concerns, 19–20, 83–87
    stereotyping, 47–49, 71–72, 89
    urban culture of, 35–39
Al Aqsa Martyrs' Brigades, 33
al-Islam, Hezb, 92, 95
Al Kapone (rapper), 37
Al Shabaab rule, 93
Alcohol and sexualized lyrics, 62–63
Allende, Salvador, 30
Allstars (rap group), 37–38
Amp'd Mobile, 46–47
Anabaptists, 31
Argentina, 30–31
Ataiyero, Kayce T., 45–50
Atlantic, 17–18

B

Banks, Tyra, 70–71
Banner, David, 36
Bennett, William, 19

Bjerke, Rebecca, 75–76
Black Entertainment Television (BET), 48
Black Eyed Peas (pop group), 63, 65
Black Gold Edutainment, 15
Black stereotypes, 47–49, 71–72, 89
Blues music, 35–39, 80–81
Boogie Down Productions, 26
Boston Globe, 8, 60
Boycotting music, 88–91
Brewer, Craig, 37
Burnside, R. L., 35

C

Cam'ron (rapper), 20
Capobianco, Ken, 60
Caramanica, Jon, 62
Carter, Kelley L., 63
Censorship
    balance in, 7–8, 32–33
    boycotting music, 88–91
    deprivation issues, 93–94
    disadvantages of, 30–31
    misogynistic lyrics, 23–27
    music lyric violence, 33, 75–77
    music under pressure, 33–34
    overview, 23–24, 29–30
    parental guidance, 27–28
    public demand for, 26–27
    revolution against, 95–96
    in Somalia, 92–96
    tyrants and, 31–32
Chad, Scarsdale, 18

Chappelle, Dave, 13
Chavis, Ben, 53, 54
Chile, 30
China National Orchestra, 33
Chuck D (rapper), 36, 51, 71, 90
Cloonan, Martin, 32
Coltrane, John, 81
Common (rapper), 41
Conscious rap, 44
Cosby, Bill, 78–79, 81
Culture and Media Institute
  (CMI), 61
Cyrus, Miley, 66

D

Daily Telegraph, 65
Def Leppard (music group), 8
Dickinson, Cody, 37, 38
Dixie Chicks (music group), 33
DJ Babu (rapper), 36
DJ Kool Herc (rapper), 56
DMX (rapper), 36, 37
Drake (recording artist), 63–64
Drugs and sexualized lyrics, 62–63
Duey, D.J., 15
Duke lacrosse scandal, 46, 47

E

Estrella, Miguel Angel, 30–31
Explicit lyrics
  banning of, 61–62
  drugs/alcohol and, 62–63
  messages in, 65–66
  overview, 57–58, 67–68
  profanity, 58, 63–64, 70
  sex and, 58–60, 68–69
  in videos, 64–65

F

Facebook (online social network-
  ing site), 9
Filthy Fifteen artists, 8
First Amendment, 7, 75
Fitzgerald, Ella, 80
Flannery, Mary Ellen, 10–16
Fletcher, Ben, 65
Flo Rida (rapper), 61–62
Flocabulary, 15
Foxx, Jamie, 58, 63
Free speech rights, 8, 83–86
Freemuse, 31, 32
Frere-Jones, Sascha, 17

G

The Game (rapper), 36, 86
Gangsta rap, 14, 24, 41, 44, 74, 81
Garowe Radio Station, 93
Gaye, Marvin, 81
Genocide, 79, 86–87
Gore, Tipper, 7–8
Gramsci, Antonio, 19–20

H

Hagelin, Rebecca, 8
Hall, Marc, 7
Hall, Rebecca, 47
Hassan, Amar, 33–34
Helping Our Teen Girls In Real
  Life Situations, Inc.
  (HOTGIRLS), 67
Hilton, Paris, 70
Hip-Hop Association, 12
Hip-hop lyrics
  activism through, 43–44, 68
  Black stereotypes in, 47–49
  blues and, 36–38

defined, 68
evolution of, 38–39
as exploitive, 46–47, 49–50
history, 14
lack of substance in, 41–43
misogyny in, 52–53, 69
overview, 35–36, 40–41, 45–46, 51–52
positivity in, 69–70
profits from, 54–55
sex and, 68–69
solving problems with, 43
"Hip-Hop Project"
(documentary), 55–56
Hip-Hop Summit Action Network, 21, 53
Holiday, Billie, 29
Howlin' Wolf (rapper), 37
Hua Hsu, 21
Huang An Lun, 33
Hughes, Langston, 11

I

Ibrahim, Mohamed (Sheik), 92–93
Ice T (rapper), 85
Imus, Don, 23–25, 52, 55, 83–87
International Covenant on Civil and Political Rights (UN), 32
Iranian Ministry of Culture, 33

J

Jackson, Jesse, 26
Jara, Victor, 30
Jay-Z (rapper), 21, 52–53, 86
Jazz music, 80–81
Jean Grae (rapper), 26
Jeremih (singer/producer), 59–60
Johnson, Robert, 36, 38–39

Jones, Paul "Wine," 35
Judas Priest (music group), 8

K

Kanye West (rapper), 11, 41, 42
Keisha (porn star), 61
Khan, Nida, 51–56
Kid Cudi (rapper), 62
Knoploh, Sarah, 57–66
Kuti, Femi, 34
Kweli, Talib (rapper), 25, 41–42, 50

L

Lady Gaga (pop singer), 57–58, 61, 65
Latifah, Queen (singer/actress), 26
Lee, Chris, 64
Little Walter (rapper), 36
LL Cool J (rapper), 14, 67
Los Angeles Times, 60
Ludacris (rapper), 11, 14, 54
Lukashenko, Aleksandr, 34

M

Madonna (music artist), 8
Makeba, Miriam, 30
Mallory, Tamika, 54–55
March for Hip-Hop Decency, 54
Marino, Nick, 35–39
Marshall, Patti, 61
McGruder, Aaron, 25
McWhorter, John, 17–22, 40–44
Mediabase, 58
Melle Mel (Hip-hop musician), 27
Milton, Little, 35
Misogynistic lyrics, 23–28, 52–53, 69

Mohamed, Kassim, 93
Montgomery-Glinski, Sarah, 12, 15–16
Morton, Jelly Roll, 80
Mos Def (rapper), 41, 42, 44, 50
Mugabe, Robert, 34
Music lyrics
    as empowering, 70–71
    meaning of, 7
    misogyny in, 23–28, 52–53, 69
    parental guidance with, 27–28
    positivity in, 25–27
    teen pregnancy, 78–79, 81
    See also Explicit lyrics; Hip-hop lyrics; Rap lyrics
Music lyrics, educational
    effectiveness of, 20–22
    entertainment vs., 18–20
    overview, 10–12, 17–18
    in school, 11–13
Music lyrics, racist
    against African Americans, 19–20, 83–87
    free speech and, 84–85
    genocide and, 86–87
    overview, 83–84
    radio station rights, 85–86
Music lyrics, violent
    boycotting, 90–91
    censorship and, 33, 75–77
    jazz/blues lyrics vs., 80–81
    overview, 7, 73–74, 78–79
    reality vs., 79–80, 81–82
Music Television (MYV), 61
Music under pressure, 33–34

N

Nagesh, Gautham, 18, 20
National Action Network, 54
National Public Radio (NPR), 76

National Rifle Association (NRA), 82
Neal, Mark Anthony, 48
Nelly (rapper), 49
Neo-Nazi music, 32
Neruda, Pablo, 29
New York Times, 62
New Yorker, 17
Nickelback (pop group), 66
The Notorious B.I.G. (rapper), 10–11

O

Obama, Barack, 20–21
Of Mice and Men (Steinbeck), 14
The O'Jays (R&B group), 81
Omar Dahla, Mohammed, 93, 95–96

P

Pandora (online music site), 65
Parental guidance, 27–28
Parents Music Resource Center (PMRC), 7
Patton, Charlie, 37
Peters, Russell, 13
Policinski, Gene, 7
Political music, 33–34, 41
Polter, Julie, 29–35
Pornography, 8–9, 48
Poussaint, Alvin, 78–79, 81
Poverty, 30–31, 37–38
Powers, Ann, 60–61
Primack, Brian A., 58–59
Prince (music artist), 7
The Prison Notebooks (Gramsci), 19
Profanity, 58, 63–64, 70

Protest rock, 26
Public Enemy (Hip-hop group), 14, 26, 36, 51, 85, 90

Q

Queen Latifah (singer/actress), 26, 55–56

R

R. Kelly (rapper), 48
Racism concerns. *See* Music lyrics, racist
Radio station rights, 85–86
Raising PG Kids in an X-Rated Society (Gore), 8
Rap lyrics
    activism through, 43–44
    conscious rap, 44
    crime and, 32
    as educational tool, 69
    evolution of, 38–39
    free speech and, 84–85
    gangsta rap, 14, 24, 41, 44, 74, 81
    poverty and, 37–38
    record companies and, 55–56
    shock rap, 85
Rappaport, Alex, 15
R&B music, 80–81
Reality shows, 71–72
Recktenwald, Adam, 13, 15
Record companies, 55–56
Recording Industry Association of America (RIAA), 7–8
Religious music, 31, 33
Rezayee, Shaima, 34
Rodman, Sarah, 8
Rosenberg, Alyssa, 18
Ross, Justin D., 88–91

Run-DMC (rapper), 67
Rutgers women's basketball team, 23–24, 52

S

Salt-N-Pepa (rap group), 67
Samad, Anthony Asadullah, 83–87
Saxton, Jessica, 92–96
Schumacher, Geoff, 73–77
Science Daily, 65–66
Searcy, Yan Dominic, 78–82
Sexualized lyrics. *See* Explicit lyrics
Sharpton, Al, 26, 54
Shock rap, 85
Simmons, Russell, 8, 21, 53, 54, 84
Sitomer, Alan, 11–13
Smith, Anna Nicole, 23
Snoop Dogg (rapper), 39, 48, 54, 77, 85
Somali Arts and Culture Foundation (SAAC), 94
Somalian censorship, 92–96
Son House (blues singer), 37
South Africa, 30, 31
Spears, Britney, 60, 70
Spelman College, 48–49
The Spinners (R&B group), 81
Stanley, Tarisha, 48–49
Steigerwald, David, 20
Steinbeck, John, 14
Stereotypes, 47–49, 71–72, 89
Stokes, Carla, 67–68
Summitt, Krista, 47

T

T-Pain (rapper), 63
Taylor, Sean, 79

Teen Mania Ministries, 75–76
Teen pregnancy, 78–79, 81
Thomas, Dylan, 11
Trew, Jonathan, 32
Tupac Shakur (rapper), 11, 36, 42, 43

U

United Nations (UN), 32
Universal Declaration of Human Rights (UN), 32
Uruguay, 30–31
USA Today, 60, 63

V

Videos, 64–65
Village Voice, 46
Violence concerns. *See* Music lyrics, violent

W

Waayaha Cusub (rap group), 94
Wald, Elijah, 38–39
Walker, T-Bone, 36
Waters, Muddy, 38
Whitlock, Jason, 79
Williams, Juan, 76–77
Willis, Bruce, 55–56
Women and Hip-hop lyrics, 23–28, 45–56, 52–53, 69
Wonder, Stevie, 81
Wynter, Leon, 21

Y

Young Jeezy (rapper), 36
YouTube (online video site), 64

Z

Zimbabwe, 34
Zimring, Franklin, 81
Zylbergold, Bonnie, 67–72